WILLIAM BOOTH IN AMERICA

Six Visits 1886–1907

R.G. Moyles

CREST BOOKS

The Salvation Army National Publications

Copyright © 2010 by The Salvation Army

Published by Crest Books
The Salvation Army National Headquarters
615 Slaters Lane
Alexandria, VA 22313
Phone: 703/684-5523
Fax: 703/302-8617

Major Ed Forster, Editor in Chief and National Literary Secretary
Judith Brown, Crest Books Coordinator
Lisa Jones, Cover Design

Available from The Salvation Army Supplies and Purchasing Departments
  Des Plaines, IL – (847) 937-8896
  West Nyack, NY – (888) 488-4882
  Atlanta, GA – (800) 786-7372
  Long Beach, CA – (847) 937-8896

Printed in the United States of America

Library of Congress Control No: 2010933306

ISBN: 978-0-9792266-9-4

Contents

Acknowledgments

I wish first to thank Major Ed Forster who encouraged me to write this book. He has been very receptive to my ideas and very supportive of the work of Salvation Army writers. To Susan Mitchem and Scott Bedio at the Salvation Army Archives in Alexandria, I owe a debt of gratitude not only for their help in finding information but for their friendship during our research time at their beautiful facility. The various staffs at the Library of Congress in Washington, D.C., Booth College Library in Winnipeg, Canada and the Heritage Center in London, England, have been, as usual, very gracious and helpful. I would also like to thank Ms. Kathy Carlisle and Major Paul McFarland at the Salvation Army Adult Rehabilitation Center in Bladensburg, MD for their hospitality and friendship during our brief time with them. And, finally, to my wife Ada, who has been my research assistant and proofreader, my eternal love.

Introduction

In 1912, not long before William Booth "laid down his sword" (on August 20), his long-time friend and promoter, William T. Stead, paid him an eloquent tribute. General Booth was, Stead wrote, the one man of his day "who has been seen by the greatest number of human eyes, whose voice has been heard by the greatest number of human ears, and who has appealed to a greater number of human hearts, in a greater number of countries and continents, not only more than any man now alive, but—thanks to the facilities of modern travel—than any man who has ever lived upon this planet" [*Fortnightly Review*, 1912: 1043].

At first glance, that might seem an exaggeration. But consider the facts. William Booth, throughout his tenure as General of the Salvation Army (1878–1912), traveled more than half a million miles promoting his evangelical and social mission; he visited more than 16 different countries around the world, some of them as many as eight times; and, by a rough estimate, he preached more than 10,000 sermons to as many as 15 million people.

Few Victorians, if any, could match those accomplishments. And when we remember that the "facilities of modern travel" to which Stead referred were mainly ships and trains—a transatlantic crossing at its fastest taking more than a week—we are left in awe at the magnitude of General Booth's vision and the strength of his commitment.

Of one thing we are certain: William Booth did not travel for pleasure. Indeed, he seldom found much pleasure in the travel itself. He went abroad because he believed in universal salvation—that the Salvation Army, of which he was the founder and spiritual head, and which by the late 1880s had planted its flag in countries as far away as India and South Africa, would be God's instrument to redeem the world in both a spiritual and social sense. He traveled, therefore, with a specific mission—to evangelize the world.

The reason why William Booth believed this to be possible was the startling fact that, by the mid-1880s, the Salvation Army was the fastest-growing revival agency in the world. By transforming his small East London Christian Mission into a military-style organization complete

with officers and soldiers in full uniform, by doing away with conferences and committees and assuming sole and full command, and by re-
naming his mission "the Salvation Army" in 1878, William Booth assured
a success even beyond his own expectations. Within a decade his Army
was attracting as many as 500,000 people to meetings each Sunday in
corps as far removed from each other as Whitechapel, London and
Bombay, India. By 1890, as well, he had launched his *Darkest England*
social scheme, creating a vast network of reclamation projects that
would make the Army one of the world's leading social-reform agencies.
Clearly, the Salvation Army had encircled the globe.

It seemed, therefore, and William Booth fully believed it to be so,
that his Salvation Army would become a religious and social panacea.
And it was to instill that vision in his followers that he traveled throughout the civilized world—to promote its efficacy as widely as possible.
He would, he reasoned, rally his troops, making sure they understood
his principles and purpose. He would everywhere preach his message of
personal salvation, and he would meet every influential person he
could—from Theodore Roosevelt to the Emperor of Japan—to encourage public support for his many social ventures.

Oblivious to all distractions—taking little interest in such natural
wonders as Yosemite or the Great Barrier Reef—he was single-minded
in the pursuit of his ambition. "The world for God" was his only ideal.
As George Scott Railton put it, "his every movement, the reports of his
journeys, the conversations he held with all whom he met, everything
told in the one great War, helped to create, more and more all over the
world, this force of men, women and children, pledged to devote themselves to the service of Christ and of mankind."

And so in any particular year—say July 1891 to February 1892—
William Booth might be found evangelizing Australia, New Zealand,
South Africa and India; in another—say the summer of 1896—he
could be heard preaching the gospel in the larger cities of Norway,
Sweden, Denmark, Germany, Holland and Switzerland; and in 1886,
1894, 1898, 1902 and 1907, the general criss-crossed North America,
preaching salvation, promoting the Army and seeking support for his
many social ventures. The world was his platform and North America
was a key part of it, growing in importance at the turn of the twentieth century.

The Salvation Army had taken hold in North America, in both the
United States and Canada, in the early 1880s and the two countries

seemed to William Booth to promise a full bounty of Salvationists and to be a vital cog in his mission. He therefore visited both countries more often than any other—six times between 1886 and 1907—advancing the Army's mission in all their major cities from St. John's to Vancouver, from New York to Los Angeles, and as far south as Alabama.

In a previous book (published 2006) I described William Booth's six visits to Canada. In this book, I offer descriptive accounts of his visits to the United States. I do so partly to understand the nature of the visits themselves—why the general thought it fit (or necessary) to visit the United States at those particular times. But I do so, as well, to gain a sense of just how the Army changed from one visit to another, how William Booth was received by the American public on each occasion, and, perhaps most important, to catch a glimpse, through newspaper reports, of his preaching style and his sparkling personality.

General Booth's first visit in 1886 was primarily a reparation effort, designed to restore public confidence in the Army after it had been torn apart by the secession of its commander in the USA, Thomas Moore, in 1884. The Army was in sore need of the general's unifying influence, and it proved to be an efficacious one indeed. During his second trip in 1894-95, the general, having become a well-known social reformer, was intent on promoting his Darkest England scheme. Just four years earlier he had published his famous manifesto, *In Darkest England and the Way Out*, to which the world responded with great favor, and now, with his social welfare programs established in most major cities, he needed to make sure that public support (in this case, American public support) should continue and increase.

In 1898, William Booth was in the United States again to help unify his forces and rebuild public support after the damaging defection in 1896 of the American commanders, his son and daughter-in-law, Ballington and Maud Booth. They had been very popular leaders, both with Salvationists and influential members of the public, having built the Auxiliary League to more than 6,000 members. So thoroughly American had they become in their nine-year tenure, that just a few years earlier they had taken out American citizenship. Reluctant to leave, they had decided not only to secede from the Army but to establish a rival organization, "The Volunteers of America," and in doing so had taken quite a few Salvationists and many public supporters with him. William's presence again helped boost morale and solidify support for the new commanders, his son-in-law, Frederick Booth-Tucker, and his daughter,

Emma, who had set the Army on a new course as one of the nation's foremost social welfare agencies.

William Booth's visits in 1902 and 1907 were less focused than the previous three and were intended mainly to "spiritualize" the nation and to enhance the organization's reputation as "the Army of the Helping Hand." There were, of course, some specific practical purposes—furthering the Army's "farm colonies" and introducing his "University of Humanity" plans—but they were, in essence, part of William Booth's effort to advance his long-held program of universal salvation.

When we look at William Booth's reception on those six visits we see a pattern of acceptance that ranged from extreme wariness in 1886 to open adulation in 1907. In 1886, both William Booth and his Army were relatively unknown to Americans—indeed, in some places, the Army was openly reviled—and thus the newspapers were skeptical of his intentions. In 1894 they were highly appreciative of his new social scheme and treated him with great respect. This, in the later visits, turned into what can only be termed "veneration," made evident by the facts that both in 1902 and 1907 the general was asked to pray at the opening of the U.S. Senate's daily session and was tendered an official reception by President Roosevelt. It is not an exaggeration to say that, by the time William Booth made his farewell speeches in 1907, he was greatly loved by the American people.

That transition from blatant skepticism to guarded acceptance to open adulation is exciting to witness. Just as interesting is the parallel change in the Army itself over the two-decade time frame of the six visits. As an organization it shifted gradually from being solely an evangelical mission to one with an integrated dual mission. In time the social wing began to become self-sustaining and certainly, in the eyes of the public, became the Army's *raison d'etre*. Along with that change, we can also see through succeeding visits a significant change in the Army as an evangelical agency: Salvationists in 1907 were a much different group from those who met William Booth in 1886, fast becoming much more self-sufficient and church-like.

Among the most delightful features of William Booth's visits to America are the personal glimpses we get of the man himself. We not only marvel at his stamina as he traveled across America and his energy as he preached or lectured as often as three times a day (usually for an hour and a-half each time), but we learn something of his personal habits—of his preference for a vegetarian diet, of his insistence on absolute quiet in his meetings, and of the demands he made on his personal assistants. We can also sense the flavor of his sermons, sometimes quoted in full by some newspapers, and we can share, through them, his intense enthusiasm for and his dedication to his mission—that of saving souls.

William Booth was a unique individual. He was strong-minded as well as single-minded, sometimes a little difficult to please, but always a tireless campaigner, full of a burning desire to save people from their sins and rescue the world from its social inequities. Through an examination of his visits, we gain a fuller appreciation of the man and his mission.

Visit 1: 1886

Re-establishing the Salvation Army

General Booth at the end of his meetings in Chicago asked the people to "cease looking at the Salvation Army through a mist of ignorance and doubt, to get closer to it, to grasp its soldiers by the hand, and learn their stories from their own lips. You would imagine," he said, "that we were a blasphemous, fanatical, hare-brained set if you believe all you heard and read about us. Come close to us and you will find something beneath the red jersey and under these hallelujah bonnets."

Chicago Inter-Ocean (1886)

1886 Itinerary

New York City, Sept. 26, 1886

Canada Sept. 27-Oct. 28

Jackson, Mich. Oct. 29

Chicago, Ill. Oct. 30-Nov. 2

Kansas City, Kan. Nov. 3

Travel Nov. 4

Dayton, Ohio Nov. 5

Columbus, Ohio Nov. 7-8

Massillon, Ohio Nov. 9

Pittsburgh/Allegheny, Pa. Nov. 10

Newcastle, Pa. Nov. 11

Scranton, Pa. Nov. 13-14

Shenandoah, Pa. Nov. 15

New York City Nov. 16
[business only]

Lawrence, Mass. Nov. 17

Lewiston, Me. Nov. 18

Augusta, Me. Nov. 19

Fall River, Mass. Nov. 20-21

Boston, Mass. Nov. 22-23

Danbury, Conn. Nov. 24

Asbury Park, NJ Nov. 25

Washington, DC Nov. 27-29

Frederick, Md. Nov. 30

Plymouth, Pa. Dec. 1

Albany, NY Dec. 2

New Brunswick, NY Dec. 3

Brooklyn, NY Dec. 4-5

New York City Dec. 6-10

Depart NY Dec. 11, 4 a.m.

Chapter One

When William Booth paid his first visit to the United States in the late fall of 1886, the Salvation Army which he had founded eight years earlier was still virtually unknown to most Americans. And most of those who knew it did not take it very seriously. Some of them ridiculed or disparaged the "new-fangled" religion, referring to Salvationists as a "wild set of religious fanatics who actually make themselves ludicrous and ridiculous." Others described their meetings as "hysterical" and questioned whether such a "wild" religion could at all be successful: "the men who talk glibly of a 'real hallelujah spree,' led by 'Shouting Annie,' are not the men to promote good order and decorum; they will never make the drunkard sober, the rowdy peaceful, and the brutal humane."

Quite clearly, even though the Salvation Army had been almost seven years in this country, in 1886 it was not, in the eyes of many Americans, anything more than a rabble-rousing religious eccentricity.

STAUNCH OPPOSITION

So strong was the antipathy to the Army that in several American towns it had been banned from the streets. In Cleveland, for example, where 24 Salvationists were arrested for disturbing the peace, a judge had declared, "The Salvation Army has become a nuisance, and must be suppressed like any other nuisance." In Wilkes Barre, Pennsylvania, Mayor Sutton, even at the moment of William Booth's visit, had ordered the Army to refrain from marching on Sunday nights, in defiance of which several Salvationists were charged with disorderly conduct and committed to the Luzerne county prison.

Similarly, in Joliet, Illinois, on January 19, a Salvation Army march (already having been prohibited by the mayor) was "raided" by the police, the officers found guilty of defying the city's ordinance, and "fined accordingly." And, in Pittsburgh, just a year before William Booth visited, a corps soldier had been attacked by "roughs" and beaten so badly that he made it only as far as the penitent-form before he collapsed and died.

TERRA FIRMA

This is not to say, however, that the Salvation Army had made no progress. In spite of such opposition, it had. Since the Shirley family—Amos, Annie and their daughter Eliza—had laid the groundwork by unofficially commencing Army meetings in Philadelphia in 1879, and since this had been built on after George Scott Railton and his seven "Hallelujah Lasses" had been sent to officially open the work in March 1880, more than 40 towns and cities had been "invaded" and a substantial number of soldiers enlisted. Most promising was the fact that, by that time as well, more than 100 local Salvationists had become full-time officers, adding to the nearly 100 who had been sent from England to push the work.

BROKENNESS

When William Booth made his first visit in 1886, the Salvation Army had still not been accepted into the mainstream of American religious life. A major reason for this, in addition to its unorthodox methods, was that in late 1884 an internal dispute—called by some a "rebellion"—threatened to undo whatever progress had been made. By 1886, the Army had not fully recovered from that near-disastrous event and, according to some commentators, was not likely to do so. It was William Booth's intention, in coming to America, to make sure that it did recover.

Though the causes of the "split" were complicated, they stemmed from the fact that Major Thomas Moore, who had taken command of America in 1881, had encountered some difficulties regarding ownership of Army property and had decided, contrary to William Booth's expressed wishes, to incorporate the Army as a requirement of American law. This he did on October 21, 1884. As a result of Moore's action, William Booth, fearing the move would somehow wrest the Army from his control, immediately sent out Commissioner Frank Smith to "take back" the Army. By doing so, he transformed what seemed like a reasonable action on Moore's part into what could only be called a "rebellion." For in January 1885, when confronted by Smith's demand to restore all property, Moore decided to keep all Army assets, rename the organization "the Salvation Army of America" and assume the title of "General."

Moore's actions almost completely toppled William Booth's small Salvation Army work in America. Many corps, such as at Schenectady, New York, one of the most thriving in the country, were torn apart, with half its members supporting Moore and half supporting Smith. Other corps (the majority, say most historians) joined Moore, while still a few others rejected both parties and set up rival evangelical units of their own.

NEED FOR CREDIBILITY

"To the few American Salvationists still loyal to General Booth," writes Herbert Wisbey, "the future looked dark indeed." For Moore had not only garnered the support of many American officers and soldiers, but owned all "the property, supplies, and equipment of the Salvation Army and had the sole right to the uniforms, the *War Cry*, the flags, the official insignia and even the very name 'Salvation Army'" [*Soldiers Without Swords*, p. 56]. It would be a difficult task to restore the Salvation Army—now referred to as the English or world-wide Army—to a position of credibility in the eyes of watchful Americans.

Frank Smith, the new commander, certainly tried hard, and, all things considered, made remarkable strides towards recovery. With the help of 50 new officers sent out from England, the brilliant but somewhat unorthodox commander began the process by opening up new corps in places not impacted by Moore's rival organization, and by launching two new social ventures—prison work and women's rescue. The former initiative attracted new converts and won back some who had defected; the latter helped restore the public's confidence, gaining Smith a prestigious audience with President Grover Cleveland. As one historian points out, Smith, in spite of his brusque style and intolerance of the defectors, "proved to be an excellent 'organizer and publicist' and within his two and half years in the United States increased the World-wide Salvation Army's corps from 17 to 143" [Taiz, Lillian, *Hallelujah Lads and Lasses*, p. 37].

ACCEPTANCE AND UNITY

What was clear, however, was this: though Frank Smith had carried the day, and though William Booth's Army soon began to cast Moore's "Salvation Army in America" into the shadows, in 1886 the organization was still struggling to achieve legitimacy. The American public—and American Salvationists—needed to be assured that the real Salvation Army would remain an active religious force and become an even more aggressive presence in mainstream American society.

In addition, American Salvationists (those still loyal to William Booth) not only needed to have their morale boosted but, as important, needed to understand that only William Booth's idea of soldiership and altruistic evangelism would be tolerated. In other words, they were to accept the fact that the Salvation Army in America would be in full accord with that in England and not simply become an "Americanized" version. These were the primary motivations prompting William Booth to make his first visit to America in October through December, 1886.

William Booth's tour of the United States began in Jackson, Michigan on October 29 after he had been in Canada for a month (Sept. 27-Oct. 28). Though this might, at first glance, seem to have been an inauspicious place to begin, it was, in fact, ideal. For not only was Jackson conveniently close to General Booth's last Canadian stop at Woodstock, Ontario, it was also strategically important, being one of the corps recently opened (Feb. 1, 1886) as part of Frank Smith's rebuilding agenda.

SMALL-TOWN REVIVALS

The Jackson corps was, as such, an example of what the Salvation Army in the United States would try to be—not merely a big-city slum mission but a small-town revival agency. It was Smith's intention to "drive into" as many towns as possible—to cover the map with small revival units that could later be built into thriving corps. It was a strategy that seemed a viable means of countering the negative impact of the Moore defection, and many small corps such as Jackson, Michigan, were giving proof of its effectiveness.

It was at Jackson, then, that William Booth, having crossed over the border in Detroit (which did not yet have a corps), had his first taste of

American Salvationism. With James Dowdle, the "saved railway guard" as extra preacher and James Vint, an accomplished musician, as his personal secretary, he took the small city by storm. It was, stated the *Jackson Daily Citizen*, "a gala day for Salvationists." For in addition to the local corps, officers and soldiers had congregated from all over the state—Port Huron, Lansing, Mount Clemens, Charlotte, Eaton Rapids, Albion, Lowell, Hillsdale, Corunna and Mason—swelling the procession to about 400 soldiers.

There were, as well, two brass bands: one from East Liverpool, Ohio, and another from Grand Rapids. The latter, stated Smith in his *Salvation War in America*, "is a very precocious band indeed," having only had three weeks' practice, but whose "uncommon proficiency was to be accounted for by the fact that nearly half the band was made up of hallelujah lasses" (p. 18). "What do you think of it?" asked the *War Cry* reporter. "Quite a novelty, is it not? There was perhaps never anything of that kind in the Salvation Army before."

DEFINING THE MISSION

After the usual supper at the local barracks (having "tea" was as much an Army trademark as its open-air meetings), the contingent staged a torchlight parade to the Jackson Opera House where, having paid an admission of 10 or 25 cents, more than 1,000 people had congregated to hear General Booth speak on "the Salvation Army in All Lands." It was a description of the Army's beginnings, a definition of its purpose, a defense of its methods, and, for the general, an attempt to win people to his cause. It began, of course, with music and singing—some selections by the band, a few Army songs, a solo by Commissioner Dowdle and a prayer—always to let people know that this was a religious occasion. And then William Booth spoke for an hour and a-half.

WILLIAM BOOTH'S STORY

"This is my first opportunity of addressing an audience in the United States," he began. "I shall be glad to say something this evening that would make any one here love their God more and their country more, which also means more love for their fellow man. There is no denying that there is a great prejudice against the Salvation Army and I would like to see it removed, and when the people know what we are doing, I think it will be removed" [*Daily Citizen*, Oct. 30].

"I was," he continued, "an ordained minister in the Methodist Church, and was doing evangelical work 26 years ago in London. One day I was led, providently I now believe, into the part of London that is the cesspool of iniquity. I was horrified at the condition of the people and still more when I was told that within one square mile of where I stood were one million people who by their actions had never heard of God, or at least did not follow his teaching. The churches were taking up money and sending it to India and Afghanistan for the conversion of the heathen, and were unmindful of the millions of people right at their door without religion.

"I thought something could be done for these people, and began to do something for them. Get a man to look at hell and keep on looking for some time, and ten to one that man won't want to get there and will want to get away from it. Every man makes an effort to save himself some time or other. Show him a glimpse of heaven and he will try to go there. So I went to work without a plan of action, with only a resolution to do good if I could. My work has branched out into the Salvation Army."

In typical fashion—with a sprinkling of anecdotes and occasional touches of humor—William Booth kept his audience entranced. He teased his listeners a little by stating that though so far "our work has been with the lower classes," he was certain that the Army was suitable for all classes, meaning most of those who had come to hear him. He made them laugh by suggesting that the hardest people to convert were the newspaper reporters. And he defended the Army's methods by stating that if anyone objected to them, all they had to do was "show [us] how to reach [the lower classes] by a kid-glove plan and we'll adopt it."

MAN OF THE HOUR

For the audience the man was it. And, as so often would be the case, the reporters were delighted to describe both his features and his gestures. "He is," wrote the Jackson reporter, "a tall man, above six feet, spare features, and wears his hair long, frequently running his hands through the gray locks when speaking, and leaving them in a disordered condition. His beard, long and gray, is untrimmed and untrained . . . His uniform was blue, with the regulation red Jersey jacket, over which he wore a handsome blue Prince Albert coat, beautifully embroidered on the chest in military fashion.

"On the collar of his coat is the insignia of his rank, a beautiful rosette, worked in red and gold. His speech is broken, sometimes disconnected, and when interested drops his h's, but when speaking more cooly gives the letter."

It was, by comparison with the many descriptions that came later, a poor one, but it set the tone for the tour and gave Americans their first journalistic glimpse of the "man of the hour."

After convening an "all night of prayer," at which Colonel Dowdle presided and at which "scores rushed into the pool for cleansing and pardon," General Booth conducted officers councils before leaving Jackson at 11:35 a.m. the next day. "The public was pleased and profited by the visit," wrote the *War Cry* reporter. "The soldiers were blessed, the officers, and in fact all were more firmly fixed and settled in their love and devotion to God, the general and their work." It was indeed an auspicious beginning.

Chapter Two

William Booth left Jackson the next morning for Chicago. The Salvation Army in Chicago was the symbol of the organization's new big-city beginning in America. A little more than a year earlier, in January 1885, Captain and Mrs. William Evans, who had come to America with Frank Smith, had scouted the city and found it ripe for a Salvationist invasion. From the moment they held their first meetings, in Bush's Hall at the corner of North Clark and Chicago Avenue on March 1, a segment of the public—not all of them "drunken men and women"—were drawn to the Army, and the work grew rapidly, encouraged by Commissioner Smith's close oversight and his concerted efforts to see that it did so.

By early November 1886, therefore, when William Booth made his visit, the Salvation Army in Chicago had given promise of a great work ahead. Salvationists were, as the old phrase has it, on the *qui vive* with excitement and anticipation. For Chicago was indeed the brightest star in Frank Smith's new regime, and it seemed entirely appropriate that William Booth should make it the first prolonged stop on his celebrated tour. In a four-day campaign that was a happy mixture of "salvation" meetings, public lectures and officers councils, he made his greatest impact on the American public.

STOPPING IN MICHIGAN

Before proceeding to Chicago, he arrived at the Michigan Central station on Saturday afternoon, October 30. The "dingy old station" was transformed into a bright display of torches and banners. "The forces [of the Army]," wrote a Tribune reporter, "were drawn up on a line along the platform. The women, in black poke bonnets, jingled tambourines, the men waved torches or hammered on drums, and amid a storm of 'Thank Gods' and 'Hallelujahs' the train pulled in [Oct. 31, p. 9].

"Greeted by Commissioner Smith and Captain Evans, and installed in a horse-drawn carriage, William Booth joined a procession to the Princess Rink for a meeting of welcome and praise. With four drums ahead and then a squad of sisters followed by the carriage, the band, and the Army, the procession moved down Lake Street, up State, and across Washington. The general stood up in his carriage, waved his canary-colored gloves, shouted 'Hurrah for Jesus!' and sat down. The band played on and the Army, about 200 in all, sang:

'Hurrah, hurray, hurrah for Jesus,
As we go marching to glory.'" [*Tribune*, Oct. 31, p. 9].

That march was "assuredly a mighty affair," stated the *War Cry*. "Three quarters of an hour's march, three quarters of an hour's drumming, music and singing, three quarters of an hour of angry merchants, scared horses and infuriated agents of the rum and other respectabilities, only served to freshen our comrades up for the great gathering at the Rink" [Nov. 20, 1886].

CHAOS

When the Chicago Salvationists arrived at the Rink for a "praise and worship" meeting, they found the Opera Room filled to capacity. According to the *Chicago Tribune*, "there was a fight for admission, and in a minute every foot of standing room on floor and gallery was crowded. People began to get frightened in the crush, and fears were expressed that the gallery would fall. Most of the 1,200 people in the hall wanted to get out, and about 3,000 outside wanted to get in. During the confusion the ticket-takers were thrown over the bannisters and one of the side doors burst in. But these little annoyances didn't disturb the meeting in the least. All through the confusion the drums beat, and the cymbals twanged, and the trumpets blared, and the tambourines jingled, and scores of leather-lunged and iron-eared soldiers, male and female, shouted or sang an excruciating parody on 'Climbin up de Golden Stairs,' to the effect that:

'When I begin to doubt,
Jesus drives the devil out.

Climbing up the golden stairs.
When I begin to fear,
Jesus takes me by the ear,
Climbing up the golden stairs.'

HALLELUJAH OVEN

"Somehow or other General Booth and his staff, and the brass band from Ohio, and Commissioner Smith and his staff, managed to get into the hall and up on the already crowded platform. The general was received with all the noise that the Army could possibly create. The drums were thumped with fists as well as drum sticks, women jumped in the air and screamed with joy, men danced and jumped and violently clapped their hands and shouted at the top of their voices, the Army flags were flourished over the audience, and the waving of handkerchiefs made one think of a month's washing on the lines in a hurricane . . . As General Booth took his seat the band played [an] old-time negro melody.

"'Marching Thro' Georgia' was then sung with a spirit that would make 'Sherman's Bummers' green with envy. Half a dozen other parodies were sung and yelled by the crowd, while every instrument played its loudest, and the women's black scoop-shovel hats with their red 'Salvation Army' ribbons bobbed and swung in time to the music" [Oct. 31]. Whatever doubts that reporter may have had about Army methods, the Salvationists of Chicago made it abundantly clear that religion (at least the kind they enjoyed) was not a melancholy thing."

As for General Booth himself, he maintained, as he would throughout his visit, a hectic round of activity. On the Sunday following his initial reception, he preached at three meetings: morning, afternoon and evening. On Monday he convened officers councils, urging them to "Take Care"— of their bodies, for God had given them to use for the salvation of souls; of their minds by being careful what books they read; of their souls by holy living; and of their soldiers, not by coddling them, but by finding them plenty to do.

It was, stated the *War Cry*, a session "in the 'hallelujah oven' (and a hot oven it is, I can tell you, when the general happens to be the stoker"). This was followed in the evening by a public meeting, during which (in a one-and-a-half hour lecture) William Booth outlined, with plenty of anecdotes and personal experiences, the rise and progress of the Army. And on Tuesday, his final day in Chicago, the general officiated at the laying of a cornerstone for the new Salvation Temple and in the evening, after a "gigantic march," concluded his visit by preaching at a "wonderful heaven-on-earth" meeting.

A DERISIVE PRESS

It seems, thus far, that most Americans were quite curious about the Salvation Army. And by his magnetism and charm the general had brought thousands to a new understanding of its methods and mission. We may also assume, as the *War Cry* confidently asserted, that new friends and new converts were made as a result of his passionate preaching and an articulate defense of his organization's flamboyant practices.

As gratifying as that was, however, it was quite clear that the "voices of public opinion"—the nation's newspapers—were not yet willing to accord Salvationists much respect. In its choice of epithets, for example (words like "leather-lunged" and "iron-eared") the *Chicago Tribune* made it quite apparent that it looked with some disfavor on Salvation Army antics. And when it did report the general's reception in Chicago, its reporters tended to focus on what it considered the Salvationists' "bizarre" behavior and tried always to exaggerate it for humorous effect. A case in point is the *Chicago Tribune's* report of the cornerstone-laying ceremony on Tuesday, November 2:

"One hundred and fifty women, men and boys, with drums, tambourines, and other inquisitional instruments, stood on a platform covering the lot where the barracks were soon to be. On the corner of Chicago Avenue and Franklin Street is the Grace Evangelical Lutheran Church, and in this the Salvationists held a private meeting. After a bit General Booth, Commissioner Smith, and Colonel Dowdle came out and the Army formed in line, and with noisy, unlovely music marched up and down the main streets of the Seventeenth Ward.

TRY AGAIN, SISTERS!

"Reaching the church, General Booth, with his hands in his pockets and his red waistcoat prominently displayed, made a prayer and then gave the history of the Salvation Army. 'It was started to save souls,' said he, 'and souls it has saved. [Hallelujah!] Money is of no consequence—the sisters will now take up a collection.' Only $7.50 was raised. 'Well, well,' said the general, rubbing his nose, 'this is very bad indeed. Isn't Jesus C. worth more than $7.50? Try again, sisters.' So the sisters tried again and raised $1.90 more.

"'H'mph,' said the general, rattling the tambourine, 't'aint very much, but we can't all be Miss Petrulia Johnsons [the major donor towards the new building].' Miss Johnson was a thin young woman, with fluffy bangs, and she smiled at the general and sighed. 'Miss Johnson will lay the cornerstone,' said the general, and Miss Johnson came forward and spread on the plaster. The stone was lowered, but the chief seemed worried.

"'What's the matter?' asked General Booth. 'She got four inches o' plaster on the end an' one on de udder,' said the mason. 'Hist 'er up again,' ordered General Booth. So the stone was set again. The building is to cost $45,000, and Miss Petrulia Johnson contributed $7,500. The rest is yet to be raised by the efforts of the lads and lassies of the Army. The exercises closed with a song to the air of 'Won't you tell me, Mollie darling?'

> Won't you tell me, Jesus darling,
> That you'll save my soul from sin.
> For I love you, Jesus darling,
> You have made me white within [Nov. 3]."

Six O'Clock Supper

With similar condescension, the same newspaper reporter wielded his pen to deride another very popular Army activity.

"After the 'holiness meeting' in the Princess Rink yesterday afternoon a banquet was given above-stairs in the cozy closet known as the opera-house. Neither General Booth nor any of his 'staff officers' was present. The general cut his wisdom teeth long ago, and not on salvation sandwiches either. The soldiers tramp through the streets, beating drums; but the general rides in a carriage. His carriage, to which were hitched two strapping horses, stood in front of the rink when the holiness meeting dwindled to an end. The general got in, followed by his staff, and was whisked off to a six o'clock dinner. Somewhat saddened at his departure, the soldiers went for the sandwiches.

"There were six tables, seating about 75 in all. Sandwiches, coffee with sugar and coffee without, cake with frostin' an' cake without frostin', baked beans, pickled and unpickled, formed the bill of fare. Someone prayed. He told the Lord that the food was all consecrated. 'It was given by the blessed sisters [hallelujahs], an' the yeast as is in the bread is the prayers of the sisters, an', O Lord, may it make salvation rise in 'em as eats it.'

"The lucky ones fell to and used knives and forks—principally knives—in a way that promised little for the 'second table.' The sisters bustled about with sandwiches, praising God and spilling hot coffee on the soldiers' legs. There was a great deal of confusion, laughter and shouts. Now and then one might notice a young brand snatched from the burning surreptitiously squeezing the hand or waist of a female brand of the same sort. It made no difference, however. The female brand only cried, 'Glory to God!' and piled an extra sandwich on his plate . . . When they were finished the baskets of fragments gathered up wouldn't have kept a canary alive two days."

CONDESCENSION

As for General Booth himself, the *Tribune* reporter said, "He has few ideas of any force, and his language is barren as well as ungrammatical. And yet when he claps his hands, stamps his foot, and shakes his grey hair down over his flashing eyes the audience is carried away with enthusiasm; women weep, men shout like maniacs, and the brass band— if it could only be born again and born dumb!—plays away like mad. The general is so big and powerful, and so energetic that the audience takes it for granted he must be saying something. The Princess Rink was well-filled yesterday afternoon, and the meeting was 'spot cash' at that. The sawdust-covered floor, the Chinese lanterns, and noisy band suggested the circus as much as anything else, and the exercises were somewhat on that order" (Nov. 1).

Since we know full well that General Booth, though possessed of a gravelly voice and speaking a low-class diction, was witty, quick to supply an original anecdote, ready to poke a little fun at himself or the audience, and was especially graphic in his accounts of the damnation awaiting sinners, it seems this reporter was intent on casting him in as poor a light as possible. But even when the overall impression was positive, the image was not always flattering.

FURTHER CRITICISM

A writer from the *Chicago Advance*, for example, wrote this about him: "He is an elderly man, of strong build and good presence, but with a hoarse, guttural voice, which detracts much from the effect of his speech. He stammers much and constantly repeats his sentences. But he speaks with great directness and was sufficiently interesting to secure the attention of the vast congregation." This reporter was, on the whole, disappointed with the Army's methods. "We came away," he wrote, "feeling that religion had suffered in the hands of its would-be friends, and that a great many people in the audience left the room farther away from the kingdom of heaven than ever" [Nov. 4, 1886, p. 708].

Such reporting (derisive if not openly negative) was typical of how the major newspapers treated William Booth throughout most of his visit. While crowds thronged to hear him, newspaper reporters, on the whole, were not at all kind. Theirs was, for the most part, a tongue-in-cheek kind of reporting, most of them preferring to highlight what they perceived to be the extravagant features of Salvation Army activity, more interested in its eccentricities than in its real message. They liked to focus on the unusual testimonies of "Hallelujah Jim" or "The Rustler," and always took every opportunity to deride the general's attempts to raise money.

THE GENERAL'S REJOINDER

William Booth's first reaction to such negative (or at least disparaging) reports was, as it had nearly always been, to dismiss them in amusing references to hard-hearted newspapermen. "We expect," he told an audience, "to get the newspapers on our side; we have converted two reporters since coming to America: they are awful hard nuts to crack. We expect to get the editors soon: they are harder still." And he jokingly referred to them as horse flies that "pass over all the sound animal and settle on a little sore. So reporters pass over all the sound, good points, of a question, but if they see a sore spot, out come their books and pencils, and down it goes."

In his private moments, however, he expressed concern that "the papers have been awfully down on our meetings," and he knew that if the Army were to gain a positive image the press would have to be courted and cajoled into a more positive attitude. Perhaps, with time, and a closer acquaintance, the newspapers would come to understand the real purpose of his mission. Such a hope, however, was only occasionally gratified. For when the general left Chicago on November 2, to travel west to Kansas City, newspaper jocularity turned nastier than it had been before.

Chapter Three

To have taken a train to Kansas City, a 500-mile-ride from Chicago, for a one-night meeting, and then, at 7 a.m. the next morning, board another for a 700-mile return trip to Dayton, Ohio, might seem to have been a waste of energy. But, again, William Booth was willing to undertake the grueling journey in support of Frank Smith's new initiative to rebuild the Army in America. For, as the *War Cry* pointed out, Kansas City had only been opened 11 weeks earlier, and in an 11-week period from July to August, the Army had opened 12 new corps in what they called the new Kansas and Missouri Division.

The Salvationists there were much in need of their leader's inspiration and support. Especially so since, at the same time, Moore's "Salvation Army of America"—so often confused in the public's mind with William Booth's Salvation Army—was also making inroads in the same part of the country. The public therefore needed to be able to distinguish between what Salvationists referred to as the "true" Salvation Army and the "false" one (Moore's "Salvation Army of America").

SCATHING DENUNCIATION

Though General Booth received a warm reception in Kansas City, where almost 200 soldiers from around the division and several hundred citizens turned out to hear him speak, it was here that he encountered his severest opposition. Not only did some of the clergy of that city meet to denounce the Army, but its main newspaper, *The Kansas City Star*, printed a scathing denunciation of the general and his methods.

The report, picked up by many newspapers throughout the country, began by stating that "General William Booth, of London, the head and founder of the Salvation Army, who has been trying to stir up enthusiasm in the interest of his organization, and no doubt to fatten his exchequer in this city, left for the east yesterday morning. When General

Booth stood before the audience assembled at the Music Hall Wednesday night to hear his lecture on 'The Rise and Progress of the Salvation Army,' attired in his customary red-flannel jacket and well-worn black satin cloak, there were probably very few there who knew that he was worth £5,000,000 and had an annual income from the harvests of the Salvation Army of about $1,000,000. Though that is not generally known, it is nevertheless the fact."

CHARGES OF DECEPTION

The reporter went on not only to detail where the money was coming from, but to discredit William Booth's autocratic control, the Army's "Orders and Regulations" (the so-called "secret book"), and the obvious aim of keeping the Army a Booth-controlled enterprise ("There shall be no heroes in this Army but Booths"). Most damaging, perhaps, at a time when General Booth was ardently seeking the support of local clergy across the nation, was the charge that he was "hoodwinking" them, teaching his officers how to deceive them: "To make ministers and others engaged in church work friendly you must dwell upon the fact that we attack those who are quite outside of their range, and that for want of education amongst us we cannot be in competition with them."

"GRIPPING" HIS AUDIENCE

William Booth had, of course, encountered such criticisms before—many of them more virulent. His consistent answer to them was this: when people hear you, and see you in action, they will know that half of what is written is a distortion of the truth. And, as he made his way east to Dayton, Columbus and Massilon, Ohio, and then into the coal-mining areas—the "black country"—of Pennsylvania, he began to prove the value of this philosophy.

In the city of Pittsburgh, for example (then often referred to as Pittsburg/Allegheny), which was almost obscured by a "dense smoke that rose up from a maze of furnaces which burn and flare among the rugged scarred hills," William Booth faced one of his toughest audiences and won them over.

"Here," wrote Frank Smith, "the general came before a critical audience; it was a case of the glories of days gone by. For, unfortunately, through the conduct of those who have gone out from us, the work has had a setback. Nevertheless, there were a faithful few who stood by the old flag. Prejudice, there was plenty; but the general has forced his way in 20 years of warfare, through stiffer and more inveterate prejudices than those which confronted him in Allegheny. He seized the occasion and the crowd with tact, force, and the fearlessness begotten of deep, personal conviction in the high and holy cause in which he was laboring; and his confidence in God and the truth was justified by the gratifying, spontaneous responses of his hearers . . . At first he gripped them, then he held, and finally he carried his audience with him, as he does all audiences who have admiration for genuine enthusiasm, and heart or soul for the cause of God, or sympathy for suffering humanity" [*The Salvation War in America*, 1886-1887, p. 27].

Growing Receptivity

In spite of the negative newspaper reporting, William Booth was, by the sheer force of personality and preaching, beginning to win new friends to the Army's cause, counteracting the subversive influence of the rival "Salvation Army of America," and beginning to dispel the myths concerning his purpose and practice. Still, he was known to say with reference to poor press, "my nightly prayer is of thanksgiving to God that I am for a time free from the devil and the reporters."

In fact, as he neared the Eastern seaboard, General Booth began to sense a growing receptiveness of his message and of the Army itself. One of the reasons for this was that, in places like Boston and New York, the Army was much better known, and had more assuredly asserted its permanence. Even though it had lost some public credibility when Thomas Moore defected, and was still looked at in some quarters with suspicion, it was nevertheless widely tolerated and, to some extent, respected.

Many New England clergymen, for example, had been to England, where they had attended Army meetings and had brought back positive assessments, sometimes based on the opinions of such noted English clergymen as Archdeacon Farrar and Reverend Randall Davidson. In addition, many major religious newspapers on the east coast—the *Evangelist*, *Zion's Herald*, the *Independent* and *The Watchman*—had carried vivid descriptions of Salvation Army meetings and activities, all quite positive.

AN AFFIRMATION

The *Independent* had this to say of the Army in August 1882: "A chief secret of the success of the Salvation Army is found in the constant effort of the leaders to keep the meetings lively. They are not disturbed by the fear of irreverence, but they are afraid of dullness. By hymn, prayer and ejaculation the congregation is kept in a state of constant excitement, which often rises to enthusiasm . . . The lesson for our churches to learn from this is the necessity of avoiding dullness. Even in the Episcopal churches, which provide for responses, how few can be got to say 'Amen' audibly, while a Presbyterian or Congregational church would be shocked if an earnest brother should speak the word which Paul expected every worshiper to repeat in unison with the public prayers."

Equally important was the fact that the Army had attracted to its ranks several well-educated young people—among them the Vassar graduates Susie and Elizabeth Swift, described as "two sisters from a wealthy, cultured home." Their conversion and soldiership made news around New England, prompting a positive article on Salvationism by another graduate of the Boston School of Theology, Katharine Lent Stevenson, who later became one of America's leading temperance advocates.

EMOTIONAL APPEAL

In her article, published in *Zion's Herald* (Jan. 28, 1885), Stevenson eloquently chronicled her initial misgivings about the Army. But, persuaded by the conversion of her friends, she attended and became one of their staunchest supporters. She wrote: "One who has known, in even the smallest degree, the power of the Holy Ghost, cannot fail to recognize that power in others; and the Army, as represented by its Boston leaders, shows forth that power. You feel it. You *must* feel it. Simple, broken words; uncouth dictions, rude grammar, and undue absence or presence of aspirates; nevertheless, back of it all, under it all, through it all, you *feel* God."

Such positive publicity and glowing endorsements went far to ensure a much warmer reception for General Booth in such places as Lewiston and Augusta, Maine; Boston and Washington, D.C.; Frederick, Maryland and Albany, New York. In Boston, for example, on December 9, the general was invited by the Evangelical Alliance to speak to an audience of about 300 ministers and Christian workers of Boston and vicinity. In his address, he took a very diplomatic approach, aware that his seeming unorthodoxy was what kept many other clergymen from offering their practical or moral support.

"Now, in anything I have to say," he began, "I don't want for a moment to speak in any dogmatic way. I don't come here to tell you how to reach people or even to advise you how to do this, but I come to tell you what I have done, as an agriculturist who, by some plan or method, might have been able to raise larger crops, would come to talk about his methods to his neighbors. I will tell you of the religious methods of myself and mine. You can consider them and adopt them if you choose.

"In the second place, I want to say that I am not assuming that we Salvationists are any more devoted to God's work than are the laborers in any other part of the vineyard. In the third place, I don't wish to say that all our methods are exclusively our own. I have no doubt that many things that we do have been done and are done now. Neither am I to assume that we have solved the question of how to reach the people we aim to reach. We have only reached the fringe of the garment as it were" [*Boston Globe*, Nov. 23].

NOTHING TO HIDE

General Booth then went on to describe, as he had done so many times, how and why the Salvation Army came into existence, the vicissitudes of the work, and its obvious successes. He ended by saying: "I am willing to admit that there are many imperfections among us, but I do claim that we are as a people honestly intent upon a certain kind of work, and that there are thousands of men and women willing to stand any amount of suffering and contempt to save a certain class of people. Even if we had failed utterly, we should still be deserving of the sympathy of every-one present. As you well know, I have no character, no reputation, and it is well known that if I am not a crank, I am next door to being a fool. Very well, I say; anyway, so long as the work is successful, we have noth-ing to conceal from the world" [Ibid].

Just two weeks later, General Booth was again enlightening as large an audience of clergymen in New York City. At the local YMCA he main-tained that "if all the ministers had a message from God that unless they got the world saved within a given time—say 50 years—they would be shut out of the Kingdom of Heaven, he thought they would all band to-gether to bring about its salvation in the best and most rapid manner, and the system which he believed they would be led to adopt would be that of an army, after the methods of the Salvation Army.

"'The North', continued the General, 'conquered the South by means of men who were ready to die, and the ministers should pick out the best people who were likewise ready to die for Christ's sake, to fight in their salvation army. They would be no good unless they were willing to die.' He would like to see such a step taken, and when it was, he hoped that they and the Salvation Army would march to-gether for the conquest of the world (loud applause). To make a raid on the enemy, argued the general, and burn his house, secure his cat-tle, and destroy everything, was a very easy matter; but to establish a fort and hold it, was quite another thing, but still this was actually the thing the Salvation Army was doing everywhere" [*Independent*, Dec. 10, 1886].

A LIGHT IN THE NORTHEAST

Though the addresses themselves were well received, and elicited loud applause, it was in the question-and-answer sessions that General Booth revealed his true nature—his quick wit and common-sense. It seemed, in fact, that, in spite of his meager education and weak theology, he was more at home among the "divines" of Boston and New York than among the lower classes of Chicago. The former seemed to appreciate his can-dor, his lack of religious sophistication, the simplicity of his message, and the enormous achievement of having brought into being a world-wide revival agency that promised to outshine Methodism itself. And, it was in such company that William Booth shone.

Exchanging Banter

To the question, "If the churches were to follow the same system as the Salvation Army, would they be as successful?" he replied with a twinkle, "They would all be Salvation Army then," the implication of which was not lost on the audience as it laughed loudly at the response. Another gentleman asked if William Booth thought "Christ was coming with the holy angels in a very short time." Again he was greeted with laughter when he said, "I don't know; cannot tell."

A minister of the Episcopal Church enquired if it would be possible for the Salvation Army to reach the higher classes; for there were a large number of high-class sinners in the fashionable churches. In reply, the general said: "In the Salvation Army we have some people who have given up all ease and luxury, and come into the Salvation Army, being anxious to reach this class of sinner," but still he was afraid that it was a hard nut for even the Salvation Army to crack. "If, however, we had a large reinforcement from the middle classes, we might, perhaps, harass the rich sinners to death. Or," he added, "to life."

Another minister (obviously wishing to make his point obliquely) asked the general if St. Paul used tambourines and drums and trumpets. "No," he replied, "but I never heard that St. Paul did lots of things that the Boston ministers do today." In reply to a question whether, if a soldier wanted to be baptized, he would allow him to be, the general said he should send him to the nearest church. "A Baptist church?" asked a voice. "Yes, a Baptist church," was the answer, "for they have all the appliances ready." To which answers, exhibiting a rare quick-wittedness, the audience laughed heartily and applauded loudly.

Throwing Bombshells

That the whole assembly seemed (at least theoretically) supportive of William Booth's mission was evident at two important moments, according to the report in the *Independent*. In the first, a woman said that as the Army was partly composed of both men and women, she thought she would be excused for saying a word: "'I have stood on the platform with Mrs. Booth, and she is a splendid helper to the general. And I have stood by the side of La Marechale Booth in Paris, and daughters of the general. He may well be proud of them.

"'I will say that every word General Booth has said is true, and surely you dear Christians are not going to stand back and not give the Salvation Army the full sympathy of your kind hearts, for if ever there was a work of God, it is the Salvation Army work, which is the power of the Holy Ghost. The churches, for example, in Scotland, are very cold, and the Salvation Army has come amongst them, and as it were, has thrown bombshells amidst them. The Church of England has approved of them and has started a church army. Never had I understood real Christian martyrdom until I saw the Salvation Army, and I think the lives and money of Christians ought to be given up to God the same as in the Salvation Army.'"

VOTE OF CONFIDENCE

The second important moment was a final benediction on William Booth's work. The venerable Dr. Lowery rose to his feet and said, "with a voice that trembled with emotion: 'I wish to move as the sense of this congregation, that we have heard with perfect satisfaction the statements of General Booth and that the Salvation Army is worthy of the sympathy of all Christian churches in New York and the United States.'

A moment of impressive silence followed it.

"'I second it!' shouted a voice at the back. 'Let us carry it with a rising vote,' exclaimed another, and in an instant the whole of the audience rose to their feet en masse.

"'Let the opponents rise,' said Dr. Lowery. None rising to their feet, the doctor turning to the general said that the vote was carried; and all who know how hard the general has toiled and fought, will understand a little how pleased he was for once in a way to receive the encouragement from his brethren in New York, more specially as just now the enemies of the Salvation Army have been very assiduous in speaking slanders and libels" [*Independent,* Dec. 10].

Chapter Four

It was quite clear, given such expressions of public support as that proposed by Dr. Lowery, that William Booth was making significant progress in making the Army's mission known. He was able also to deflect some of the criticism being leveled against it, and to counter some of the negative influence of the recent "troubles." It was just as gratifying to know, however, that Salvationists themselves were rallying around the flag—that many of those who had briefly flirted with Moore's version were returning to the ranks of the "true" Army. The founder could feel a fresh breeze of optimism and the Salvation Army had, he believed, weathered a severe storm and was now ready to chart a new course.

Rallying 'Round the Flag

He sensed it especially in the welcomes he received. In every town the occasion took on a festive atmosphere. They were, as the local newspapers described them, "red-letter" days, for such an infusion of music and singing, of parades with banners and bands, were rare crowd-pleasing novelties in small-town America. Not only did General Booth arrive with his own small entourage—Commissioner Frank Smith, Colonels Dowdle and Vint, and a divisional band—but they were often preceded by a contingent of Salvationists from other towns. Major Whatmore would come down from Boston with a railway carload of Salvationists; Adjutant Lampton and his contingent came from Lewistown, and, in return, when it was Lewiston's turn to host the general, officers and soldiers from as far away as Philadelphia converged on the town.

One popular "warm-up expert" was Captain Walsh, the "Saved Minstrel," who would be at nearly every event to "grease the throats" and lift the spirits. He was the "banjo man" whose maroon jersey was aptly inscribed: on the front, "Jesus Calls You," and on the back, "A Burning Hell Awaits the Careless," while on his red leather belt was the word,

"Eternity." He was colorful, he was talented; he was half mad (so said the press), and he danced and sang.

There was, to be sure, much more of celebration than of solemnity in the proceedings. But evident through all the gusto and noise there was "a sincerity of purpose, an earnestness underlying the seeming abandon, which must have been very gratifying to the commander who has come hither to lead his armies in person for a time" (*Globe*, Nov. 14).

PANORAMA

And when the "commander" himself began to speak, silence reigned. He is, continued the same reporter, "a big, tall, earnest, fiery, grand old man, with a shock of long iron-gray hair that falls to his neck like the mane of a lion. It falls to his breast in many lines and makes the warrior look like Noah when he entered from the ark in quest of a barber. Among this whirling frame of hair are a large, generous mouth, a big Roman nose and a smooth, full forehead, all telling of a man who has abundant physical strength and pluck. He is not an orator; he is not a ranter.

"Rather plain and homely in his use of the King's English, he culls his words for the force more than for beauty, and he delights in the use of saws [proverbial sayings] and idioms. The habit of dwelling upon an idea, of turning a happy conceit over and over, showing it in a new light and keeping it before the public gaze until every one must see it, is a strong one with him. When one thing is finished, he goes to the next without any connecting link, so his whole talk is a series of pictures, like a panorama" [Ibid].

THE KINGDOM IS NOW

Pictures of depraved humanity, of amazing conversions, of the awfulness of hell and the comfort of heaven. Those were William Booth's specialties. "I am a blood and fire soldier," he said, "and I can stand and say, 'thank God I'm saved.' I thank the dear Lord that I have the consciousness of that salvation which I preach, for I both preach and practice to all the salvation of the cross. It was said by a prominent bishop in England, but a few weeks back, that the Salvation Army would ultimately overflow the earth, but it was added whether the result of that overflow will be beneficial or not cannot be determined.

"On the first point I agree with his lordship, and as for the second he would need but to visit us and be with us for a short time and he would be assured that our results will be beneficial. If you can be sure there is no hell, I am sure there is a heaven. Shall I prove it to you? I have the foretaste of it in my own soul. I have found a short cut to heaven. You needn't go around the cemetery or with the undertakers, that most unfortunate of people. I have found a better way. That is not of going across the river to heaven, but by God bringing heaven over the river to us. I do not care whoever there may be in this house, whether they be Baptists, Methodists or nothingists, they are all seeking a future happiness. The workingman says when he obtains riches that happiness will be attained; the gambler says when success attends him his wishes will be gratified. But that is not the fact.

Finding Joy

"You will not obtain happiness that way. You will find heaven when you find God; you will find heaven when you find the end of the devil. O, the years you have hunted for that happiness! When a schoolboy you looked forward to a business life to give it to you. When at work you looked forward to a married life to bring it to you; and when marriage came, also came the thought that with riches I might obtain happiness. But in all that time you have searched and searched in vain. I am not preaching a heaven that you must die to reach, but one that you can enjoy here. That is what we have come to publish and what this salvation teaches" [*Globe*, Nov. 23].

Open Door

"You all ought to be blood-and-fire soldiers. There is the Baptist wing, the Methodist wing, and all other wings, and there is plenty of room. Our religion is not only to save our own souls, but to teach our people to think of others as well as themselves. We don't believe in the religion learned from books, from ministers and sermons. We believe in the religion of the soul. Our principle is, 'I am saved myself, and now I will try to save others.' If there is a great ship wrecked on the rocks of this coast, do you suppose that the persons who had friends on board would stand looking at the wreck and seeing their friends drown, listen to lectures on the subject, and examine models of vessels? I should hope not. Yet it is so in this city today. Men are being wrecked on every side. Should we look on and be simple witnesses of this, and not put out a hand to save them?" [*War Cry*, Dec 18].

Such sermons, when transcribed, seem disjointed and vapid, but when we recall, as the reports point out, the depth of feeling invested in every word, the modulation of that raspy voice, the intent look in his eye, and the tall figure swaying to the rhythm of his words, we can understand why, for an hour or more, people (in a pre-television era) were held spellbound in their seats and would be subsequently inspired to action.

SPECIAL MOMENTS

While almost every meeting with William Booth was a memorable occasion for his officers and soldiers, there were, for the general himself, occasional highlights, special moments, which either swelled his heart, gave him an intense personal satisfaction or brought back precious memories.

The visit to Frederick, Maryland, for example, was one such occasion. The meeting on November 30 was typical of most. The Opera House was "taxed to its utmost capacity to hold all who wanted to get inside, and many were content to get even so much as a peep at the stage where the general was expected to appear. The hall was already well filled when the general and his party arrived and the shout sent up when he entered was a boisterous indication of the feelings of the vast assemblage. It is safe to say that they were 2,000 people inside the building and in the halls and on the stairs.

"The Salvation songs were rendered with a vigor and vim that was only surprising to those who had never heard them before, the banners were waved as if every breath that touched their folds was sacred to the salvation cause, the drums and tambourines were beat with an energy that meant business, and the whole affair was happy and alive and jubilant" [*The Daily News*, Dec. 1, 1886].

African American Revival

After just a 45-minute sermon, however, William Booth disappeared—
he had hurried off to the "colored corps" for a brand-new religious experience. There, among 125 of the most intensely involved Salvationists
he had ever met, he felt the power of revival as he had never done before, and loved every moment. Here is how the *War Cry* described the
scene:

"We entered the barracks amid a tremendous volley, and saw hundreds of colored folks on the platform. I saw an excellent corps of colored soldiers in uniform, and in front, we saw an additional sprinkling of
soldiers wearing some emblem of the Army. A few whites are in the top
gallery, but only a few, for it had been announced that the meeting is for
colored people only. The meeting is continued with song, but there are no
songbooks; only a very few can read. However, one begins a simple song,
which the others take up, and they all get away together in the chorus:

> De good ole way, de good ole way,
> I'm trabbling on de good ole way;
> I want to go to Hebben when I die,
> Trabbling on the good ole way.

"Whilst they sing, they jump and shout for joy as the Spirit of God
comes upon them. A blessed influence rolls over the meeting, and the
glory comes down too while they continue to sing:

> I hung my sins on de gates of hell,
> Trabbling on the good ole way;
> And I said to the debbil, 'fare you well,'
> I'm trabbling on the de good ole way.

"The general quite fell into their simple ways, and offered a soul-
stirring prayer, such as they could easily follow. Then the song:

> We're climbing up Zion's hill,
> We're climbing up Zion's hill.
> Oh, my Lord, we'll soon be at de top,
> Climbing up Zion's hill.

IDENTIFYING WITH JESUS

"A time of real blessing follows as the general leads them step by step to the throne. The glory streams down, and they look to heaven with uplifted hands, whilst the tears roll down their furrowed cheeks. Fancy pictures them as they used to be in the hard times gone by, with the cruel iron chains on their poor limbs, toiling under the galling yoke of slavery. Our hearts were moved, and went out to them with the tenderest affection, and we imagined just a little how our Savior must have felt towards these poor people during their unhappy years of sorrow. But they are happy in God now. Hallelujah." [*War Cry*, Jan. 8, 1887 and *The Salvation War in America* 1886-1887, pp. 43-44].

MEETING HIS MENTOR

A second and just as memorable experience occurred just two days later in Albany, New York. In many of his lectures William Booth made reference to his conversion, and to the powerful influence which James Caughey, the well-known America revivalist, had on his life and his preaching style. He had first heard Caughey in 1846 in Nottingham, and was awakened by him to the possibilities of revivalism. Later, in 1857, the Booths again met Caughey in Sheffield, were greatly impressed by him, and had their second son, Ballington, baptized by him.

General Booth had become a Caughey disciple: he was, he told his American audiences, an extraordinary preacher, "filling up his sermons with thrilling anecdotes and vivid illustrations, and for straightforward declarations of scriptural truth and striking appeals to conscience, he had up to that time never heard his equal."

"LET ME LOOK AT YOU"

It was a pleasant surprise, then, to find that James Caughey, now 76 years old, and unable to attend William Booth's meetings, was living in Albany and had requested to see his protégé. "The meeting of these two leaders of Israel's host was most touching," wrote Frank Smith. "Mr. Caughey had been suffering great bodily affliction for some time, and was unable to be at the meeting as intended; a strange feeling came over us as the door [to his apartment] opened at our summons, and the grand old warrior for God bade us enter; we had read and heard much of this mighty man of God, and we looked upon him with reverence and love.

"With the joyfulness of a little child he led the General into his room, and turning him round to the light, said with a voice trembling with emotion, 'Let me have a look at you.' A long pause, during which his eyes filled with tears, and he said, 'Yes, the same dear face, the same look. Blessed be God for this meeting'; and then they sat facing one another and telling of God's wonderful dealings with them during the years that have rolled away since they last met; the great spiritual conflicts they had fought together in the old country were rapidly run over, and then the general rose to go.

"TAKE OFF YOUR HAT!"

"'Are you going?'

"'I must,' replied the general.

"'Too short; too short,' said the grand old warrior.

"But the public meeting was waiting for us, and we were forced to go; then, with one of those happy touches of inspired simplicity, given to great men, Brother Caughey, looking up to the general, as he was about to cross the threshold, said:

"'Take off your hat, I am an older man than you, you know.'

"And, the general, reverently obeying, received the old prophet's blessing" [*The Salvation War in America 1886-1887*, p. 45].

Like Caughey, whom he admired so much, William Booth had a gift for vivid illustration, apt anecdote, and passionate persuasion. As one reporter put it, his sermons (and each talk he gave was part lecture, part sermon) "sparkled with humor, shone with dramatic power. Intellectualism has no place in his life. Theology he leaves to the schools and the churches, and . . . metaphysics are not the path to the masses." General Booth's messages were therefore straightforward, as accessible (he liked to say) to Mary, the servant, as to her mistress: "there are three things one must have: forgiveness of the past, strength to do good in the future, and a spirit of love for others. If there is any way to get these except through regeneration by the Holy Spirit, I have yet to find it." Few who came to hear him, the local newspapers said, went away disappointed. Rather, they were stirred to emulate his example in any small way they could.

Chapter Five

By the beginning of December 1886, William Booth was nearing the end of his first visit to America. It had been a tiring (though not tiresome) experience but, after a few days rest, he was ready for his final assault on New York City (Dec. 8-10). The public reception, he knew, would be magnanimous; the crowds would be large; the enthusiasm of his "lads and lassies" would be at fever pitch; and it would, taken as a whole, indicate a fair measure of success. America had warmed to William Booth and he, in turn, had warmed to America.

The only disappointment was that some of the nation's major newspapers still remained unconvinced of his integrity. The *New York Tribune's* reference to him as "Generalissimo" was an indication of its dismissiveness, and when, in later issues, it labeled him "General Bombastes Furioso Booth" or described him as a "sort of haggard John the Baptist, pinched and fasting and crying aloud—in Cockney English—in the wilderness," one can easily see that this newspaper at least was not impressed by his personality or preaching.

And so, in terms of public exposure, William Booth's visit ended almost as it began. As he later put it himself, "one paper painted me like an angel of light, and another like an inhabitant of the other place." Some, like the *Ocean Grove Record*, were magnanimous. "The Salvation Army," its editor wrote, "despite all the sneers and jeers heaped upon its head, is the best organization this country has witnessed to break up every low combination of vice and sin, and tackle Satan on his own ground, to rescue debased drunkards, abandoned characters, and misguided infidels from his vice-like grip" [Nov. 25].

Unlike that paper, however, most were still unkind. The *Washington National Republic*, for example, describing William Booth's visit to that city on November 27 through 29, was positively nasty in its attempt to reduce the Salvationists' celebrations to a kind of orgy. After labeling the welcome a "din," the reporter went on to say that "when the noise subsided General Booth managed to jerk out a few short sentences, to the effect that his vanity was gratified much in being received so handsomely. The general is "English, you know, and says 'caunt' and 'shawnt.' He is a tall, ill-formed man, round-shouldered, crick backed, and hollow chested. Such a physical appearance evidenced not much lung power on the part of its possessor. This conclusion was correct, for the general's voice is not of the mellow, pleasing, silvery-tongued kind possessed by several prominent American stump speakers."

DISPARAGEMENT

After deriding most of the meetings, the reporter concluded with this very nasty statement: "The general moved about before the audience, exhorting them to come and kneel. He approached the reporters' stand and said to a scribe: 'Why don't you come up, instead of going to the devil?' The journalist ventured the remark that he thought the general had a good deal of assurance, but if he should ever go the devil he would no doubt find General Booth one of his Satanic majesty's most loyal subjects."

Though not nearly as nasty as that, and though giving us excellent detailed accounts of the general's final meetings in the United States, the New York papers (mainly the *Times* and the *Sun*) were also not willing to be generous in their assessment of the Army's viability or achievements. *The New York Sun*, when it reported on the general's second-to-last series of meetings on December 9, chose to do so in a most off-hand fashion. The Army, it said, held a meeting for the local clergy with the sole purpose of converting such clergymen by "sheer force of uncontrolled enthusiasm."

DR. LOWERY'S DEFENSE

What it entirely ignored was the fact that the meeting was not at all riotous, that William Booth's history of the Army was so well received that at the conclusion Dr. Lowery, who chaired the meeting, made a motion to the effect that "we are of the opinion that the Salvation Army is worthy of the respect and support of the ministers not only of New York but all over the United States"; to which the 250 ministers present gave unanimous approval. Nor was it fair enough to note that, at the evening meeting held in the Presbyterian Church, the audience was so large that the gallery, which had not been used for three years, had to be thrown open; nor that all who heard the general were deeply impressed by both his eloquence and his commitment.

A NON-STOP SCHEDULE

Next day William Booth held three meetings: a 10:30 a.m. officers councils, a 3:00 p.m. special praise meeting, a 7:45 p.m. public lecture and, to cap it off, an 11:00 p.m. "night of sacrifice" which lasted until 4:00 a.m. the next morning, giving him just enough time to catch his ship before it left at 5:00 a.m. All were again disparaged by the press. *The New York Times* described the afternoon meeting in this fashion:

"It was a little after 3 o'clock when the din began. An overture from the orchestra, which was hardly waked up, cleared the way for a young man whose lungs occupied his whole interior, to lead off in prayer. The young man paid a poor compliment to the musicians. 'O Lord,' he thundered in tones that dislodged the cobwebs from the ceiling, shook the windows and stirred the chandelier, 'we don't ask you to give us good musicians, but O Lord, make us good men.' The audience shouted 'Amen' and 'Hallelujah,' while the performer on the biggest barreled horn peered down its throat and the young man who knocked thunderous noises from the bass drum hugged it closely in his arms and looked wildly around.

"During the song that followed, which was composed of several verses of three or four words each and a refrain of 'Oh, salvation' repeated 15 times to each verse, the orchestra awoke and got to work in earnest. Out of consideration for the audience it didn't start in all at once. A youth with an accordion took the lead, followed, after an interval, by six cornets of different pitches and the bass drum. The second verse was read by Colonel Dowdle, the leader, amid the chorus of peculiar cries, and the orchestra rushed through it at great speed, leaving the accordion to wheeze out its protest in a dismal wail at the end. The next verse was explained at length by the colonel, and the cries of the soldiers were so loud that two babies were frightened out of their wits and howled disrespectfully" [Dec. 11].

AN ALL-NIGHTER

It was the "all-night sacrifice" service that especially captured the reporter's fancy. In a report titled "All Night Hallelujahs," and sub-headed "The Salvation Army Sits Up for a Frenzied Pow-Wow and War Dance," a *New York Sun* reporter, obviously delighting in his own powers of description (of exaggeration, some might suggest), gave his readers this account on the following day:

"General Booth was going back to England, and he decided to bring about a general engagement before going. The Army marched over from Steinway Hall at 11 o'clock on Friday night, after the close of the service there. Before opening the final round, as they called it, they fortified themselves well with food at a Sixth Avenue restaurant. The keeper of the restaurant says they ate an unusual number of pies, preferring mince pie to any other kind.

"Then they went to the Shiloh Church and arrayed themselves in line of battle . . . In the body of the church and the gallery were the curious hosts of unrighteous, who had gathered to see the battle, and had paid ten cents to get in for all night. Among them were several young men in dress-suits, some young men and young women who went as they would go to the Wild West show, and others who wondered whether anything would be done that would have any effect on them . . .

"At midnight General Booth took the floor to exhort his hosts before the charge. He talked for three-quarters of an hour. He stood on the floor of the church, turning from one wing of his forces to the other, letting the audience see his aquiline nose and thin grey beard in profile. He began in a low, half-chanting tone. Whenever he raised his voice, the 11 fighting captains shouted. After the general had finished, this is what happened:

FANFARE

"Major Gay played the concertina and the soldiers sang several songs. While some sang, the others cheered, moaned, and occasionally an enthusiastic soldier yelled. Commissioner Coombs talked. He was interrupted by Private Happy John, who stood up and yelled. General Booth blew a whistle to make Happy John quit yelling, and Major Fielding stood up and yelled. General Booth blew the whistle at Major Fielding when he thought the major had gone on long enough, and Captain Boor-man stood up and yelled. He unbuttoned his coat, showing his red jer-sey, and shouted, 'I never wait for God to do for me what I can do for myself.'

"General Booth said, 'Everybody sing and clap their hands. Lift up your right hand before the Lord and sing with him looking at you.' The hands went up and more songs were sung . . . Captain Sister Brown climbed on a bench and told of her experience in the wicked city of Denver. While she was speaking young captains jumped up all over the hall, closed their eyes, and made a noise like a steam-whistle going off through a human throat.

A FAINTING FRENZY

"It was about two o'clock now, and the members of the Salvation Army, we are told, were in a state of frenzy . . . The whole Army, except the workers and skirmishers, prayed out loud and sang. There was no co-herence in the songs or prayers. A group in one place would sing one song, while a group a few feet off might be singing another song. Half the women were frenzied. The skirmishers and the working captains made a direct assault on the audience. Male and female soldiers sallied out of the wings and went down the aisles. Whenever the officers pointed out a man or woman, the soldiers sat down beside him or her, put his or her arms around his or her neck, talked to him or her earnestly, and tried to lead him or her up to the platform, where the fighting majors would look after the captive and ensure victory . . .

"Some of the audience fled before the onset of the Salvation co-horts. Women were fainting here and there over the hall. Nobody trou-bled much about them, knowing that they would come to. Up in front several women had what the Salvationists call glory fits. They jumped up and down, tearing off their hats and letting their long hair stream out. Their shrieks went up in volleys. Long after three o'clock the tone of the meeting changed. There was a triumphant peal. In the shrieks of the converts at the platform there was a joyous note. Finally, with a victori-ous shout the whole Army, the converts, and many of the audience who had gone there to scoff, began to sing the song of triumph, 'I'm saved, I am, I know I am.' Finally, General Booth, at four o'clock, got up and closed the meeting" (Dec. 12).

Chapter Six

When William Booth sailed from New York on December 11, 1886, he was, as might be expected, a tired individual. In the nine weeks he had spent in Canada and the United States he had traveled 10,000 miles, spent almost 20 days—close to 480 hours—in railway cars, conducted nearly 130 meetings, almost two a day, and preached or lectured to nearly 200,000 people. It was an arduous undertaking, considering that in that span of time he had had to sleep in more than 50 different beds and eat at as many different tables.

Though his stamina and energy never ceases to amaze, we are always aware that he was human—sometimes undeniably so. His digestion, for example, was a constant bother. He ate and drank abstemiously, no meat at all, and mainly, for almost every meal, dry toast, strong tea and an apple or perhaps rice pudding. Such a diet, though not hard to provide for, must have caused many of his hosts to grumble, as often (we are told) he would send back the toast because it was not dry enough, too burnt, or otherwise not to his taste.

HINT OF LONELINESS

His letters reveal that he was constantly aware of his fragile health and how careful he needed to be not to overtire himself (not easy away from home and dependent on the good will of others). He writes to his wife, Catherine, whom he missed very much: "You need not have any anxiety respecting my health and strength. I watch carefully any indication and am anxious to come back as well and strong as can be. I see my value to the work of God and your happiness just now and shall not knowingly throw myself away. In my humble opinion, it does not matter how much I do, so that I do not go really beyond my strength. No doubt the climate at this time of year, cool and yet not too cold, and the change, brace and keep me up. Then I am really very careful, get enough sleep one way or another, and being unable to write on the train gives my brain a good deal of rest, and altogether I am careful" [Begbie, Harold, *The Life of General William Booth* (1920), Vol. II: 70].

In that passage one might detect a touch of loneliness, for William Booth was often, even in the midst of crowds, an intensely lonely man, so adoring was he of Catherine and dependent on her as well. This was his first long absence from her re-assuring presence, her moral support, and her common-sense advice. He missed her terribly.

DEAR CATHERINE

"Send me love-letters," he writes, "and particulars about yourself. Tell me how you are: how you get up and go about, and what you do and what time you retire, and whether you read in bed when you feel sad. Tell me about yourself. To know what you wear and eat and how you go out, indeed, anything about yourself, your dear self, will be interesting to me."

And in another, he interrupts his accounts of meetings and sermons to ask her to "Love me as in the days of old. Why not? I am sure my heart feels just the same as when I wrote you from Lincolnshire or came rushing up Brixton Road to hold you in my arms and embrace you with my young love." And with even more emotion he declares: "Before starting on anything else, and I have plenty before me, I must scribble a few lines to my beloved. My thoughts have been with you through the night. When I awake I can safely say my heart comes over to you, and I embrace you in my arms and clasp you to my heart and bless you with my lips and pray God to keep you from all harm and bring me safely to meet you again on earth" [*Begbie*: II: 72-73].

He was reminded, again and again—by someone who had heard Mrs. Booth preach at Exeter Hall and by many who had read her *Aggressive Christianity*—of just how well-known she had become in her own right and thereby of her importance to his own ministry. The fact that she was just now beginning to suffer from terminal cancer, which would take her life less than four years later, made the separation doubly painful.

ATTENTION TO DETAILS

It was not that William Booth had much time to be lonely; it was just that he had an immense need for personal assurance of his success. And since he did not make friends easily, and trusted hardly anyone (even his most capable subordinates) to make major decisions, he chose to carry the weight of the whole organization on his shoulders.

Therefore, when not preaching, or promoting the Army in public lectures, he was busy overseeing even the minutest details of Army business, both in America and, by letter, back home. "We must have some more divisional officers here," he would write to Bramwell. "Push it on. Look them up. Let them get here before I leave the States. Four good commonsense young fellows should come away at once."

And when he was not thinking of such basic things, he was deciding who would take over from Frank Smith as commander. His son, Ballington, who had made such a favorable impact on Americans just a few months ago, was his choice, and in his letters he asks his wife and Bramwell to make arrangements for Ballington's transfer to the United States. "It must be," he said, "an appointment for at least five years."

PRIVATE DOUBTS

And yet, in the midst of all his busyness, in spite of his adept public performance (the shaking of many hands, the small talk with many dignitaries), he was a very private person—beset by doubts, pining for the love of his adored wife, and always concerned that his efforts did not rescue as many unsaved people as they should have or that his mission was still misunderstood and publicly maligned. And, as he sailed from New York on that December morning, he must have seriously debated with himself just how successful, in terms of gaining a positive public opinion and rebuilding his Army, his visit had been.

If we judge its success merely by the newspaper reports alone, we might (as some historians have done) label it a failure or (in Roy Hattersley's words) a "fiasco." However, if we judge by the long-term impact of his visit, by the way the Army in the United States recovered from the Moore defection and, especially under Ballington Booth, began to reassert its mission, we must believe the first visit was, on the whole, an undisputed success.

Back in London William Booth sounded confident in a speech to an audience at Exeter Hall. "In the United States the vastness of the area is perfectly amazing. I rode about for hundreds and thousands of miles, and seemed to see scarcely anything at all. There are territories and states just beginning to be peopled three or four times larger than

Great Britain, with only something like a fourth or a fifth of the inhabitants of this metropolis only. Into these nations the Army is pouring forth. We have had there every kind of difficulty, yet what wonderful conquests have been made, what wonderful victories have been gained!"

SUFFERING MUCH

His comment on the Moore defection was not a kind one. "In the States," he said, "we have had to suffer from the traitorous action of the officer who was placed at the head of affairs, and who after blundering with his accounts and smashing up our work, endeavored to justify his conduct by befouling my character and the character of the Salvation Army. We have had that to suffer all the way through the States.

"Instead of sailing under their own colors they enter a town with our name at the top of their publication. They make us suffer for all the bad conduct that is so common amongst them. People have not known which was which and which was the other. I consider it would have been worth crossing the ocean 100 times to be able to meet Christian men—men who are willing to come and meet me—willing to come and inquire; who were glad to see and hear for themselves, and who when they did hear, frankly said, 'Our prejudices are swept away; our misapprehensions are gone. We believe in you, General Booth.'

"One of the most prominent clergymen in New York, at a little private gathering of ministers who met me to say 'goodbye' the night before I left, took my hand and said, 'General, come back in two year's time, and you will see another thing altogether.' So we shall before two years have passed away" [*War Cry*, Jan. 29, 1887].

A POSITIVE IMPRINT

That was said, of course, to those who fully believed it, as William Booth no doubt did. He was expected to say no less. But the evidence does show that his visit did have an immediate and long-lasting impact on the Army in America. He had gained many opportunities, especially among influential people, to give an accurate account of the Army's mission and future ambitions.

His concept of a true Salvation Army soldier had returned some soldiers who had deserted with Moore back to the fold. The future, he felt and said, promised greater gains and renewed spiritual warfare. His only disappointment was that he had to spend too much time on his first visit defending the Army against mistrust and misrepresentations. He had wanted to be a preacher—to build God's Kingdom in America—but, perhaps not unexpectedly given that the organization in Great Britain was still encountering opposition, he was forced to be a promoter and apologist.

The main fault, he felt, lay with the reporters, whose employers (the newspaper magnates) seemed determined to belittle his efforts and deny his success. Yet he also firmly believed that those newspapers did not accurately reflect the opinions of a majority of Americans. The people in general had gained a new measure of respect for the Salvation Army through his explanations and actions.

By the time William Booth made his second visit to the United States in late 1894 and early 1895, the organization had begun to endear itself to the American people—being by then actively engaged in social as well as evangelical outreach—and its members were eager to face new and more exciting challenges.

WAR CRY
And Official Gazette of The Salvation Army in
THE UNITED STATES.

No. 678. | PUBLISHED WEEKLY BY BALLINGTON BOOTH, 111 READE ST., N. Y. CITY. | NEW YORK, SATURDAY, SEPT. 29, 1894. | Entered as New York City as second-class mail matter | Price, 5 CTS.

UNCLE SAM: "WELCOME, GENERAL BOOTH, THRICE WELCOME! I RECOGNIZE THE SPLENDID SPIRITUAL WORK OF YOUR ARMY, AND BID YOU AND IT GOD SPEED!"

Visit 2: 1894-95

Selling the

Darkest England Scheme

General Booth was received with a storm of applause and a tumultuous waving of white handkerchiefs. He outlined the social scheme laid down in his Darkest England, *and now in practical operation in London, making his points by illustrations drawn from the experience of the London Army. His discourse was wonderfully brightened by anecdote, local hits and side sallies of wit. The description of the visits of the "slum angel" to a London slum was a particularly vivid bit of word painting.*

Boston Daily Advertiser (Feb. 20, 1895)

1894-95 Itinerary

Arrived St. John's, Newfoundland, Sept. 18

Toured Canada until Oct. 21

New York City Oct. 22-27

Waterbury, Conn. Oct. 29

Jersey City, NJ Oct. 30

Newark, NJ Oct. 31

Brooklyn, NY Nov. 1

Philadelphia, Pa. Nov. 2-4

Washington, DC Nov. 5-6

Baltimore, Md. Nov. 7

Pittsburgh, Pa. Nov. 9-11

Cleveland, Ohio Nov. 12-13

Cincinnati, Ohio Nov. 14-15

Toledo, Ohio Nov. 16

Detroit, Mich. Nov. 18

Flint, Mich. Nov. 19

Saginaw, Mich. Nov. 20

Chicago, Ill. Nov. 22-26

Minneapolis, Minn. Nov. 27-28

St. Paul, Minn. Nov. 29-30

Omaha and Council Bluffs, Neb. Dec. 1-3

St. Louis, Mo. Dec. 4-5

Springfield, Ill. Dec. 6

Kansas City, Mo. Dec 7

Denver, Col. Dec. 9-10

Colorado Springs, Col. Dec. 11

Salt Lake City, Utah Dec. 13

Oakland, Ca. Dec. 15-16

San Francisco, Ca. Dec. 17-20

Fresno, Ca. Dec. 21

Los Angeles, Ca. Dec. 22-24

Sacramento, Ca. Dec. 25-26

Portland, Ore. Dec. 28

Tacoma, Wash. Dec. 29-30

Seattle, Wash. Dec. 31-Jan 1

Canada Jan. 2-Feb 14

Buffalo, NY Feb. 15

Boston, Mass. Feb. 17-19

Worcester, NY Feb. 20

Providence, RI Feb. 21

Springfield, Mass. Feb. 22

New York City Feb. 25-26

Departed New York Feb. 2

Chapter Seven

What a difference eight years made. When William Booth undertook his second tour of North America, between October 22, 1894 and February 27, 1895, his mission to the world had changed dramatically. No longer was the Salvation Army simply a revivalistic agency; it had become, in the eyes of the public, a social welfare organization. Granted, its social ministry was also intended to save souls, but what the public saw were its efforts to succor the "submerged" masses—its Rescue Homes, Prison Gate Refuges, hostels and slum work.

The change had come about slowly at first as concerned Salvationists at the Whitechapel Corps in London began to care for the homeless young girls who came to their meetings. By the mid-1880s this caring had resulted in the establishment of several Rescue Homes for such young women. Encouraged by the success of that venture, in 1890 William Booth decided to make social work a permanent feature of his mission and did so by publishing his famous social manifesto, *In Darkest England, And the Way Out.*

In it he proposed the establishment of three distinct social colonies: "city," "farm" and "overseas." The first of these, already underway, would rescue men and women from the slums, provide short-term employment, and attempt to rehabilitate them for useful citizenship; the second would place some of these people on farms, teaching them the rudiments of agriculture so that they might, if satisfactory, emigrate to the third step in his program, "colonies overseas" in Canada, Australia, South Africa and the United States.

SOCIAL WORK WINS POPULARITY

The British public was, on the whole, wildly enthusiastic about William Booth's plan of social reclamation, as were most reviewers of it in Canada and the United States. Not only did people purchase some 200,000 copies of the book in the first year of publication, but, within a few months, had contributed almost 100,000 pounds towards the *Darkest England* scheme. In the United States, the new commander, Ballington Booth, had had extra copies printed to meet the great demand—a demand created by the many positive reviews of William Booth's "scheme" which appeared in almost every major journal of the day. From the *Literary Digest* to the *American Review of Reviews* to *The Overland Monthly*, from the pulpits of such famous men as Dr. Joseph Cook, from the mouths of politicians and social reformers, Americans were well informed of General Booth's ambitious plans to stem the tide of poverty and social abuse.

A NEW KIND OF MISSION

The Salvation Army, therefore, was, in the eyes of most Americans, a new kind of religious mission. "From their works and aims," wrote one observer, "the Salvationists may be called social reformers rather than religious workers intent upon spreading the faith throughout the world. Their dealings are mainly with the physical condition of humanity, preparing men for a better mental and spiritual life. They try to reach the mind and spirit through the body" [G.E. Walsh, "The Salvation Army as Social Reformer," *The Chautauquan* (June 1893): 333.] As another writer in the *Christian Union* put it, "Now, so long as the Salvation Army seemed to us to be expending itself in emotionalism, in crude testimonies and cruder music, we were indifferent to it. With the issuance of Mr. Booth's book, *In Darkest England*, the Army entered, if not upon a new stage in its life, at all events upon a new manifestation of that life, and is therefore to be commended and supported."

Though neither assessment was completely true, they were in 1894 the dominant public views of Salvation Army service. For the Army's destiny was now firmly defined: it would be a dual mission, but one which eventually would be recognized mainly as a social service agency.

SOCIAL WIZARD

In 1894, then, William Booth was no longer a mere revivalist—he was now one of the world's great social benefactors, a genius in the field of social reclamation, whose opinions on important social (and even political) questions were avidly sought and valued. He was, in fact, one of the foremost celebrities of the late nineteenth century.

And that is why, when he made his second visit to America, he was hailed as "the social wizard who would recast character and rearrange humanity," his visit being seen as one of the great moments in American life. It was also why so many prominent Americans—the Goulds, Vanderbilts and Rockefeller—were happy to chair his meetings and why, as well, most clergymen were content to support his cause. They now no longer saw the Army as a rival of the church.

As the *Decatur Daily Review* put it, "Attention and consideration is being given to the Salvation Army now that it never received before. In quarters where only laughter or scoffs were heard, praises for the Army are spoken. The visit of General Booth to this country has been made notable by the people who have received him. His statements about the work of the Army have been received with respect and given an examination that proved them to be true. The sensational methods of the Army are being overlooked by those who objected to them and the real good accomplished is being acknowledged" [Oct. 28, 1894].

FINANCIAL SUPPORT

Such immediate recognition and acceptance, such adulation, gave William Booth the freedom to presume upon his hosts' good will. (Not that he probably needed such assurance because he was, by nature, an open and blunt person). He was, he put the matter quite frankly, not merely in America to make friends—"to inform the public as to the real character of the Salvation Army"—and not even to gain moral support for his social work (though that was important). What he wanted most was to persuade people to give up some of their money so that he could take away with him as much as $400,000 to be used in the implementation of his *Darkest England* scheme.

He threw himself into such persuasion not merely because he believed in the scheme but also because his beloved wife, Catherine, had died just four years earlier (October 9, 1890). Perhaps, as his biographers suggest, it was to forget the pain and forestall loneliness that he promoted his scheme with a greater passion than he otherwise might have and why he had transformed himself into a worldwide roving ambassador for the Army's social work. It was as such that he had undertaken an eight-month tour of South Africa, Australia, New Zealand and Ceylon in 1891-92 and as such that now, in 1894-95, he would spend nearly five months in North America.

That the Salvation Army had changed considerably with the introduction of its social wing seems obvious. It is equally true, however, though perhaps not as obvious, that the American membership of the Army—both in terms of morale and social status—had also changed. When the general arrived in New York on October 23, 1894, after having spent a month selling his Darkest England scheme in Canada, he could immediately sense the improvements in both the morale of his officers and soldiers, in the changed nature of the Army's membership, and in the respect accorded him in the press.

In the first place, the Salvation Army had almost wholly recovered from the effects of the near-disastrous desertion of Commander Thomas Moore in 1884. The general's own visit in 1886 had speeded up the process, already set in motion by Frank Smith, but the hard work of the new commanders, Ballington and Maud Booth, who had succeeded Smith in 1887, accelerated the restoration process. With more winning personalities than Smith's, Ballington and Maud built more intimate relationships with their officers and won the hearts of many influential Americans. And, being more conciliatory than Smith, in 1889 they welcomed back many former officers (including Richard Holz and Emma Westbrook) who had joined the ranks of, but had become disenchanted with, Moore's "Salvation Army of America."

THE AUXILIARY LEAGUE

Their greatest achievement, however, one mainly attributable to Maud's efforts, was the creation of an Auxiliary League of influential, and often wealthy, Americans who pledged themselves to support the Army's work. "A woman of passionate sincerity, charming, quick-witted and graceful," writes historian Edward McKinley, "Mrs. Ballington Booth presided over the drawing-room meetings of the League in an elegant uniform 'of fine material and neatly made' and a bonnet 'trimmed with broad silk ribbon,' sometimes alone, sometimes with a slum officer, a singer, or an instrumentalist.

Rich and Famous

"Women were so affected by her accounts of the Army's 'great work of reclaiming drunkards, rescuing the fallen, and saving the lost' that they wept, opened their purses, and even donated their rings and jewelry on the spot" [*Marching to Glory*, p. 61]. By 1896 more than 6,000 League members—among them such celebrities as Josiah Strong, Lyman Abbott, Frances E. Willard, Chauncey Depew and Mrs. W.K. Vanderbilt—were pledging their five dollars, in return for which they received a year's subscription to the *War Cry*, tickets to all Army functions, and a badge, which signified their membership.

These leading citizens were willing to support the Army because they saw that William Booth's social plans were being implemented in very obvious and practical ways. Maud Booth had taken personal charge of the rescue of young girls from prostitution and had opened Rescue Homes in several cities such as Brooklyn, Oakland, Grand Rapids and Los Angeles. The Army's "Garret, Dive and Tenement Brigade" was, if not flourishing, at least making a significant impact on the slums of New York. And in December the Army opened the first of its cheap food and shelter establishments, calling it the "New York Lighthouse."

And that was why, inspired by Maud Booth's passion for the poor, so many influential people became Auxiliary League members—not merely as a "social fad" (as one newspaper put it) but as a token of genuine interest and respect. It was why, also, so many of Wiliam Booth's afternoons, in the larger cities at least, were devoted to meetings for auxiliaries and friends. At one such meeting, in New York, Dr. Josiah Strong, one of the city's best-known preachers and writers, stated that, "I have been converted to the bass drum and the cymbal. General Booth is the only British general in more than 100 years whose commission has conferred upon him any authority in the United States." To which the more than 500 auxiliaries said "Amen!"

Mirroring Society

The second most noticeable difference in the American contingent was that the membership itself had, to a large degree, become more stable and slightly more middle-class. The people to whom the Army

ministered—the abject poor and the down-and-out—were not always
the ones who became soldiers: the bulk of its membership was composed of working-class people, with quite a few from the professional
classes. That trend, in 1894, was accentuated by the fact that the evangelical branch was becoming separated from the social, and the corps
were becoming religious communities unto themselves, much as other
churches had.

Therefore, the Salvationists who met and feted William Booth in
1894 were not, on the whole (although some of them were), from the
lowest social classes, but were representative of American society itself—some low, some high, with most in between. This was a factor
noted especially by one of America's most popular news magazines,
Harper's Weekly, when it reported on the initial meetings in New York
on October 22 and 23: "The boxes in the balconies [of Carnegie Music
Hall] were filled with clergymen and laymen of consequence with their
families: and as one ran his eye along their rows he saw what perhaps
would not be visible anywhere else in the world on a similar occasion—
Salvationists sitting with their families and friends in these boxes, here
a stalwart fellow in his red waistcoat, the pride of well-to-do parents,
and there a young lady in her simple blue bonnet and Norfolk jacket beside father and mother and brother in immaculate evening attire." In
other words, the Army in America, as elsewhere, was becoming more
respectable.

ALLIES IN PRINT

The third, and certainly very happy, change was that American newspapers were now almost unanimous in their praise of the Army. No longer
did they lampoon the "excesses" of Salvation Army worship, or criticize
its aggressive behavior, but drew attention to the "cymbals and trumpets and drums, and fervent exhortations" as simply a different, but entirely acceptable, way of worshiping God. "The soldiers of this Army,"
wrote one reporter, "are human, and they never pretend that they are
not. On the contrary, they purposely impress the spectator with their animal spirits, their exuberance, and their love of life. These characteristics were especially apparent at the [welcome of William Booth]. There
was no disposition to suppress any outburst or expression of feeling;
chaffing was freely indulged in; natural wit had full play; but the most

remarkable feature of the meeting was the sudden change to sincere piety and religious fervency" [*NY Times*, Oct. 23, 1894].

More Support

Unlike 1886, when many newspapers were intent on ridiculing the Army, in 1894 the American press was decidedly on William Booth's side. The tenor and tone of the "new" reporting was much like that manifested in the Logansport, Indiana *Daily Journal*: "The visit of General Booth in this country is an event of greater interest to more people than would be the visit of any other religious leader in Europe. General Booth is founder and head of the Salvation Army, which was at first regarded by many people as a travesty of religious organization, but he has lived to see it one of the greatest powers for Christian work in Europe and America, with its influence rapidly extending to all parts of the world.

"... The work of General Booth met with much prejudice from the churches in the beginning, but it has been conducted on lines laid down by the Master himself, has reached out for the poor and the vicious to save them from themselves, and has extended Christian influence into the slums, and it has long since come to be recognized as a great work for good. It has even become the model in many things for Christian work by other agencies, and is today recognized as the work best calculated to redeem the plague spots of all great cities where churches were unable to live or be of service to the cause of either religion or humanity. The Salvation Army has become the greatest standing army in the world, and its march has ever been against the evils that drag men down" [Nov. 9, 1894].

Chapter Eight

As soon as William Booth began his tour in New York on October 22, practically the whole city "volleyed out a welcome," and it became abundantly clear that he and his mission to the poor would receive an overwhelming vote of approval. And by their very numbers and their colorful displays, his Salvationists also let America know that they, too, would be noticed. At six o'clock in the evening in Union Square they converged from various points in the city to hold what was termed "the largest open-air meeting the Salvation Army ever held on this continent." The Boston Jubilee band, in their "white duck leggings and black suits," brought Salvationists and curious followers from one direction; the national staff band from another; and several other local bands from others, the bands forming a cordon around the stand upon which the general was soon to appear.

"There were," stated the *War Cry*, "countless banners and torches fluttering over the heads of the swaying multitudes like sails and beacon lights on a wide sea. Besides these the electric and calcium lights most beautifully illuminated things in the immediate vicinity of and on the grandstand. Thereupon were stationed the national staff and the slum and rescue women warriors, each wearing a white sash" [Nov. 3].

PANDEMONIUM

When, at 6:30, General Booth mounted the platform, the welcome was deafening. The bands played, the people shouted, clapped their hands and waved their handkerchiefs. "Such a screaming, shrieking, shouting, yelling and belching of noise and sound had scarcely ever before been heard on Manhattan Island; it really seemed as if the earth would split, and that the skies would need a new roof. The commander [Ballington Booth] couldn't silence it; then the general tried his hand. He saluted, bowed, threw kisses, and held up his hands in pretended despair, but

all to no avail, until the people had all uncorked and shot off their enthusiasm, which had been so long pent up, to see their dearly beloved
general.

"When the noise ceased, the general referred to it as 'a very beautiful and musical tune,' at which everyone laughed. 'I need not tell you,'
he continued, 'that it has gone away down into the depths of my soul,
but I shall remember the music and I shall remember the voices for
many a day to come . . . God bless you all! (Loud amens). God bless
America! (Great cheering). God bless the Salvation Army! (Still greater
cheers). God bless everybody that loves God! And God bless everybody
that doesn't! God bless the world, and bring it to the Master's feet as
soon as possible! And all the people said Amen!'" [Ibid].

A MASSIVE CROWD

Almost as soon as General Booth had finished speaking, "the great sea
of humanity seemed as if struck by a sudden tempest that set it all in
commotion, and it surged like a great tidal wave towards the street cars
on Broadway and the elevated trains for Carnegie Hall." Here, wrote a
reporter for the *New York Times*, "General Booth was greeted by a
throng that, used as he is to facing big numbers, must have been an ex-
ceptional one. On the stage, tier after tier of seats was filled with men
and women of the Army. Every seat in the body of the house was filled,
the galleries swarmed with men and women, and at the rear, and for a
certain distance down the aisles, all the standing room was taken. Not a
few of the men were in evening dress, and the women with them handsomely clothed" [*NY Times*, Oct. 23].

A THOUSAND BRIGHT FACES

On the stage itself sat nearly 900 officers and a band of 116 pieces. "The
platform," wrote a reporter for *Harper's Weekly*, "was something to look
at. A thousand bright faces shining with enthusiasm; a thousand badges
of warfare against misery and sin; men in red waistcoats [actually red
guernseys] and blue coats, clerical in cut, military in ornament; banners
and flags and bright musical instruments; women in broad shoulder-

sashes, red, blue, or white; and one group of young women of the 'Slum Brigade' wearing great ginghams with 'Rescue' printed in large red letters across the bosoms; and many a sweet and roguish face framed in that bonnet which somebody has called 'kiss-me-not,' doubtless adding, under his breath, 'What a pity!' " [Nov. 3, 1894, p. 1048].

A few hundred of those in evening dress—some of them on the platform—were members of the Army's Auxiliary League. They were familiarly known as New York's "400" and among them were the Vanderbilts, Rockefellers and Goulds. It was an impressive display of public support, and when the general walked to the platform, with some of those leading citizens, "every one stood up, 5,000 handkerchiefs shook out a wild, prolonged flutter, and a sound came which drowned the platform out. To whom did this general belong, anyway! All Salvationist mouths were divided between laugh and loud amen, but those Americans, from floor to roof, sent cheer after cheer, shout after shout, wave after wave at the old lion on the platform, as if they thought him *their* general; and so we saw with great satisfaction how they received him" [*All the World*, Dec. 1, 1894].

On the following afternoon, after officers councils in the morning, the general met and talked to a large audience of Auxiliary League members. He was introduced by Dr. Josiah Strong, secretary of the Evangelical Alliance and a committed Auxiliary member. He began by saying that some people differed with the Army and disliked its methods, condemned and criticized its tactics, but, luckily, they all had business engagements "and there are none of them here." After hearty applause he continued, saying that he had been "converted to the drum, the tambourine and every article of warfare which the Army employed, so long as it obtained the desired ends of Christianity." But more, he thanked God for having inspired General Booth and given him the wisdom to "establish and lead such a host of conquerors" [*War Cry*, Nov. 10].

SIMPLE THEOLOGY

In characteristic style, William Booth then addressed the captive audience. "He explained the simplicity of the Army's theology . . . 'Our creed is simple. Any attempt to disjoin creed from conduct is fatal. We believe in heaven and hell, and we desire that what we teach should commend itself to the heart rather than to the intellect (Applause.) [The] most important [thing] is that each one should know that his sins are forgiven . . . A member of our Army in Exeter not long ago met a young dandy who had his mustache all curled up, and was dressed to kill. (Laughter).

"'Oh,' said he to the Salvation Army girl, 'you don't know as much as I know.'

"'What do you know?' said she.

"'Why,' he said, 'I can say the Lord's prayer in Latin.'

"'Oh,' she replied, 'I can go much further than that; I can say I am saved in English, and what is more, I can prove it' (Applause.)

"He and his party delayed going a little while to allow the audience to get out, but they hung on in considerable force, and when at last he had to make the start they lined the passageway from the top stair to the carriage door, doffing hats and cheering as he went through. Just as he reached the sidewalk a lady stopped him, shook hands, and slipped a diamond ring into his hand. 'Sell it,' said she, 'for the cause!' Her heart had been melted, and so she turned over to him her mite, and may God give her a brighter gem for her eternal crown!" [*War Cry*, Nov. 10].

CHAUNCEY DEPEW

In the evening General Booth gave his first lecture on his *Darkest England* scheme, one that would become the mainstay of his second tour of the United States. He could not have been more honored to be introduced by someone as notable as Mr. Chauncey Depew—railroad president, politician and one of America's foremost orators. "Mr. Depew said that it had been his lot to introduce such men as [Sir Henry] Stanley, Edwin Booth, Sir Edwin Arnold and Archdeacon Farrar, and it was always a pleasure to fill such a position. But it gave him infinitely more pleasure to introduce a man who had created a far wider force than any of these, a force which knew no limit except that of humanity itself. General Booth had reached a class of men, which had not been reached for 1,800 years. Few men deserve the gratitude of the world. Peter the Hermit deserved it, Martin Luther deserved it, and General Booth deserves it because of the permanent and enduring good which [the Salvation Army has] accomplished for the human race" [*All the World*, Dec. 1].

IN THE PALM OF HIS HAND

And then, as he would throughout his tour—in Philadelphia (where "several of the highest society ladies went round selling tickets"); in Washington, Baltimore, Pittsburgh and Cleveland; in Cincinnati (where he was met by "a little Army of real, warm-hearted Army-spirited auxiliaries, all decorated with welcome badges"); in St. Louis and the major cities of the West, and back to Boston and New York—William Booth, for at least an hour and a half each time, held the audience in the palm of his hand. If there were two public meetings (as there were in New York), he would in the first describe the progress of the Salvation Army from his conversion to the present; and in the second he would speak on his *Darkest England* scheme. If but one public meeting, Booth would deftly combine the two lectures.

IMPOSSIBLE RELIGION

In vivid illustrations he showed them the dens into which his slum sisters entered, washed, dressed and fed the starving babies. He led them to the Bank of England where, outside its doors, a young girl "has a little basket of matches, which she pleads of the hurrying throng to purchase of her, and while she is standing there in the wet and cold she is suddenly taken ill and is hurried away in a wagon to the hospital and before she arrives her child is born." He took them beneath the railway arches where hundreds spent their nights, into the Army's soup kitchens where so many were crowding to get a decent meal, into the Army's shelters where discouragement was met with hope. He led them into a narrow alley into which the sun's rays never reached and into a single room where a whole family ate, slept and died—one room where father, mother, big girls, big boys and little ones all lived. "How difficult morality must be in such a place, and how impossible religion must be there."

A HELPING HAND

Striding the platform, he cajoled his audience with humor. "If a ship were foundering off the shore would you take an organ down to the shore and play pretty hymns? (Laughter.) No! If men did not go in the lifeboat, the women would (laughter and applause). It was all very well to talk about helping the poor, but it was inhuman and unchristian to look into a man's or woman's antecedents before rescuing them. The man is down, never mind how he got down, help him up, make him get up.

"Some people find fault with the Army for not looking into a man's character. Why, if a rich man went into a palace hotel with a lady on his arm nobody would ask into his character or inquire if the lady was his wife or his neighbor's as long as he paid the bill (laughter). So with these poor men, when they come into a Salvation Army hostel, they put down their two cents and get their lodgings, just like in any other hotel."

Or he might, as he often did, recite, in his inimitable style, one of his favorite poems:

> When a cab-horse falls upon the street,
> No matter who's to blame;
> If carelessly he missed his feet,
> They lift him just the same.
> The sunken of our fallen race,
> A tenth is not a few;
> We'll lift them up in every case,
> When the general's dream comes true.

> In the grand old book of books we read,
> God made him from the ground;
> In Eden's garden he did feed,
> Where plenty did abound.
> But now he's starving in the slums,
> And can't get work to do;
> To the garden back we'll bring the bums,
> When the general's dream comes true.

> From the city colony to the farm,
> Transplanted Jones will be;
> And then, with rural knowledge armed,
> To the colony o'er the sea.
> Old things will pass away, you'll see,
> And everything come new;

You'll read the name, "John Jones, M.P."
When the general's dream comes true,

Oh, the general's dream, the noble scheme,
Gives John Jones work to do;
He'll have a bed, and be well fed,
When the general's dream comes true.

PERSUASIVE PASSION

General Booth was passionate: "To say that the lowliest and most wretched of human beings cannot be rescued is a libel on God, and I believe in God!" He was bold: "Lend us your money, and we'll pay you back: five percent here and 95 percent in heaven." And he was persuasive: "At Carnegie Hall $8,000 was raised towards the general's *Darkest England* scheme."

If the meeting was a "salvation" one, as it was on Wednesday, October 24, William Booth would revert to his old revivalist style, and, even though most of his audience were non-Salvationists, he would give them a "stirring-up, do-your-duty, come-to-Christ harangue":

"When we have got an article for some domestic use, say a dish; if it is polluted, we say: 'Have this dish cleansed; I cannot endure it on the table!' The sight, the smell, the taste of it is noxious to us. And if the servant comes back and says: 'This dish cannot be cleansed,' what do we say? 'Then we will destroy it!' and we smash it—cast it away from us as a thing that is hateful. God acts in the same fashion with us. He says: 'I want these men and women to honor me; I want to make them vessels of mercy, channels of salvation; I want to make them pleasant in my sight, beautiful in my eyes; I want to be glorified in them, to adorn them, to live in them, to work through them.'

"This is what He says to you who are sitting here this morning, you who are on this platform; He wants us to be worthy of Him, to be witnesses for Him in our conversation, in the way we do our business, in the manner we conduct ourselves, in the clothes we wear, the songs we sing, the testimonies we give; to witness that God lives, and that Christ enables us to be holy on earth, and filled with the Holy Ghost, to go forth on the right hand, and the left, a fire burning up evil and glorifying the great God of heaven."

FORGIVENESS OF SINS

He was uncompromising, powerful and persuasive. People might come out of curiosity to see and hear the great founder of the Salvation Army; parsons might gather by the score around the platform, or sit down to listen to what they thought might be an orthodox disquisition; and well-to-do religious folk might fill the reserved seats, with and without opera glasses, just to study what they called "the fine old man."

"But, oh my," wrote a *War Cry* correspondent, "what a surprise [they got]! Instead of the conventional 'Mr. Chairman and Christian friends, it is with a profound and unfeigned sense of gratitude that I acknowledge your greetings and will now proceed to my lecture on——,' the general rises as if he had lived in the city his whole lifetime and knew every man Jack of his audience, and taking the song-book from the leader (pro tem) says:

"'From all the sins over which I have wept, cleansing for me. Ah! Here is something substantial: cleansing! Think of it. All my sins! The sins of my youth; the sins of my manhood; the sins done in secret, in private, in public, heart-sins, hand-sins, eye-sins, ear-sins, thought-sins, open, wicked sins; all! all! all! He [the song-writer] meant more than that, too; he intended to write, "From all the SIN (not sins, merely) over which I have wept, and not wept, there is cleansing for me." 'Not only a new name, but a new nature; not only pardon of evil, but deliverance from its grip! Sing it, sing it now!'

"The general is a general," exclaimed the *War Cry* reporter. "No wasting time over the flummeries of speech: like his master, he is intent upon his Father's business" [Canadian *War Cry*, Nov. 17, 1894].

Chapter Nine

One of the pleasant surprises of this trip (as opposed to the first) was the adulation of the nation's newspapers. Reporters now flocked to William Booth's meetings and crowded his press receptions. The fact that the general was now as much a social reformer as an evangelist gave them more diverse and substantial subjects to raise, and the same diversity allowed William Booth greater scope to meet their expectations.

A QUICK WIT

He was, they noted first of all, always in good humor, was straightforward in his answers and, above all, quick-witted in dealing with unexpected situations. In Oakland, for example, he had scheduled a press conference for 11 a.m., and was not happy when no one arrived until noon, for promptness was something he always insisted upon. "When he met the press representatives," stated the *Oakland Tribune*, "he announced that they were not prompt, as his watch recorded 12 o'clock, when they had been notified to meet him at 11 o'clock." When it was pointed out to him that his watch must have gained time in crossing the continent, he quickly, and with characteristic humor, turned the mistake to his advantage: 'I guess,' he said, 'that this must be a Salvation Army watch. We are always gaining ground'" [Dec. 15, 1894].

This quick-wittedness the reporters loved, and made much of in their reports, especially when, as he often did, he made some remark to the effect that, as to the possibility of their salvation, they were indeed "hard nuts to crack." And he caused great merriment when he added that he expected their editors were the "toughest nuts" of all.

POVERTY NOT A SIN

The interview with the press representatives of the New York area when he first arrived, which appeared in various versions in almost every

American newspaper from the *Oskosh Daily Northwestern* to the *New Orleans Daily Picayune*, was typical of most:

"As General Booth sat at the big table, surrounded by reporters and correspondents, he looked the man confident of his powers without being demonstrative of that fact. He felt that he was great in the arduous greatness of things done. He is tall and wiry. Perhaps he is a trifle bent at the shoulders. Tall men often are, especially when they get to be sixty-five years old. His hair was once black. Now it is gray and projects in a long foretop brushed to the right. He runs his fingers through it nervously as he talks. He takes off his gold eyeglasses and puts them on before breathing again. He diddles with the chain from which his glasses dangle. He shifts in his chair. He is a man whose nervous energy must expend itself in more than one way at a time. For instance, a visitor to the international headquarters in London found him sitting for a portrait, dictating to two stenographers and eating his luncheon. He breaks down stenographers with overwork, while he goes on as fresh as paint.

"The conversation started on the social scheme of General Booth. Then he talked freely and with animation. 'It isn't wicked to be reduced to rags,' he said. 'It is not a sin to starve, to pawn the few sticks of furniture to buy food and pay the rent. It is a misfortune that comes to people, honest, good people, in hard times or when work is hard to get. It is such people that the social scheme means to help by getting them out of the congested towns back into the country where they can become hardy, thrifty peasantry, the glory of any nation.'

"'We do nothing for nothing. We do not pauperize by gifts . . . The essence of the scheme is that we will transfer prepared people from the over-crowded cities to a prepared place in the country. These will not be people classed as the 'submerged tenth,' but those who have been raised by God's grace from the 'submerged tenth,' or who are rescued before they go under.'

PROMOTING THE FARM COLONY

"'The essence of my farm colony scheme,' he went on, 'is the transfer of prepared persons from the overcrowded slums. These persons are not submerged, but are in such circumstances that their poverty may lead them to be submerged. Their habits may be changed so that they may help to form what I consider the glory of any country, an honest, hard-working peasantry, contented with plenty to eat, and having a happy hallelujah time of it.'

"'We are able to reform people in the city. Of the lost girls we have rescued, 75 percent have proved faithful after a three years' test. We have 102 institutions in England, including 64 slum post reserves, 48 homes for ex-criminals, 21 shelters, 33 labor bureaus and 17 farm colonies.'

When the general was asked, "'Do you think the millennium will come if the whole world is converted to the Salvation Army?' he answered, "If the newspapermen were converted it would be a very long step in that direction.'

Emotions

"The conversation turned then on the demonstrative methods of the Salvation Army.

"'There is a noisy church and there is a silent church,' said the general. 'I don't know why one shouldn't be as good as the other. Our people have not reached the point of modern culture where all emotion must be suppressed. When our people feel good they show it. If they are happy they shout. They are happy and they make no secret of it. Religion is a matter of the heart, of the feelings. I have been in churches where the people acted as if they had been made of terra cotta. It was not a Salvation Army meeting. We are uncultured in the art of suppressing our feeling. When we are happy we laugh.'

"He looked at his son, Commander Booth, and said, 'I am through, am I not?' The son, who had been hanging on every word, said, 'Yes, father,' and the general rose to go."

The Sacraments

The general at times had to walk a thin tightrope, balancing his answers to the many questions concerning matters of practice and theology, in his attempt to win friends and influence people. On the matter of the sacraments, for example, when asked how the Army stood with regard to baptism and communion, he replied: "Up to the present time it has not been practicable to have either of these in our meetings, but in the future we feel that perhaps the Lord might lead us to take a different course.

Meantime, we have constant spiritual communion with Christ, and the baptism of the Holy Spirit. If any soldier is disposed to take the wine of communion he is at perfect liberty to do so, and, so far, no church has refused to receive those who manifested this desire." It was, to say the least, a neat avoidance of commitment, but necessary to maintain the semblance of orthodoxy in the face of possible criticism. Walking theological tightropes became one of William Booth's specialties.

WESTWARD MARCH

As General Booth proceeded westward—through Philadelphia, Baltimore, Pittsburgh, Cleveland, Cincinnati, Detroit, Chicago, Minneapolis, Omaha, St. Louis and Kansas City—the tributes became more effusive, and the welcomes more elaborate. "In Philadelphia, the birthplace of the Army in America, the general had two meetings with an audience of 5,000 on each occasion. The front row of seats in the Royal Academy of Music was said to resemble a Presbyterian assemblage or a Methodist conference more than anything else. These seats were adorned by five bishops, half-a-dozen doctors of divinity, and a rabbi" [*All the World*, Jan. 1, 1895]. In Cleveland, where the Army had a thousand soldiers, the Music Hall meeting at night saw 3,500 people brave the cutting wind and the falling snow and, as a local paper stated, "thought themselves well repaid for their daring when they left the building."

OPEN ADMIRATION

In Chicago, on November 22, the reception was astonishing, the press being especially generous in its welcome. "Thousands of people," stated the *Times*, "saw the commander-in-chief yesterday morning and afternoon. Having taken one look at his grave, gentle, *wonderful* face, they decided they liked him. When they heard him speak, if it was only to say to the cabman: 'You can drive on now,' they became certain they liked him. When he turned in passing, and spoke kindly to those following, folks expressed their admiration audibly and said: 'He's a fine old chap, ain't he?' In fact, General Booth caught the town, and wherever he goes, from now until next Thursday morning, when he leaves, he can be certain of a hearty welcome. It was a grand and great picture the great evangelizer made when he came to the city. A tall, massive-boned man, with the head of a patriarch, and the face of one whose soul is very near to things divine, and whose heart is filled with a tenderness for humanity.

"Here the spontaneity of the whole campaign, the feeling of genuine affection that seemed to animate every individual at every meeting astonished and gratified our, by this time, travel-worn leader. He only reached the city at breakfast time, yet within two hours he was in the midst of over 200 press men and women in their splendid club room, allowing them to put their queries and answering them with a snap and vim that fairly enchanted them. Indeed, next day they put their feelings into words by saying that he was 'a jolly good fellow'" [Ibid, Nov. 23].

VERBATIM REPORTS

Most gratifying was the fact that the city's newspaper editors sent to every meeting a bevy of shorthand experts and printed *verbatim* every word that William Booth uttered. "Here, too, the general addressed the champion conclave of clergymen. The gorgeous Willard Hall, with its marble pillars and frescoed roof, presented a unique sight with 800 gentlemen in black broadcloth coats and white neckties. Never before, perhaps, had the general had such intelligent, eager listeners—all having apparently the utmost respect and goodwill for himself and the Army. A lady occupying a high position in the Women's Christian Temperance Union pressed her way to the platform at the close, exclaiming: 'I must thank the dear general for standing up for us women!'" [Ibid.]

GRACIOUS ESTEEM

And so the welcomes went, overwhelmingly warm and gracious. In Minneapolis (Nov. 27-28), where the Exposition Hall could not be heated to a temperature higher than 10 degrees below zero, some 2,000 people sat for over two hours in furs, overcoats and hats, "so charmed by the general's bravery that they almost forgot their uncomfortable surroundings." In St. Louis the novelty was a dollar dinner sponsored by the Commercial Club at which nearly 200 merchants sat down to a meal and gave the general a chance to address them on the economics of his *Darkest*

England scheme. "The general was delighted with his audience as he had long wanted to meet a company of hardheaded businessmen, and lay before them this particular side of his proposals."

In Omaha, which William Booth visited on Dec 2 and 3, his schedule was typical of most: three meetings on Sunday (holiness in the morning, a lecture on *Darkest England* in the afternoon and a salvation meeting at night) and two on Monday (a breakfast meeting with about 60 of the city's leading citizens and a 10:30 a.m. meeting with its clergy), after which, in the early afternoon, he boarded his train for St. Louis. The reporter for the *Omaha Daily Bee* gave a full report, prefacing his piece this way: "Omaha was proud yesterday that it had always been a friend of the Salvation Army. The city has entertained presidents, warriors and statesmen, but to none of them, though there might be more pageantry and ceremony, did it show higher honor or testify more sincere esteem than to General Booth a prophet, a preacher, a reformer, a philanthropist, who is a soldier only because sin must be fought, who is a general only because a contest against the intangible powers of darkness must have direction" (Ibid, Dec. 3).

EVOKING JULIUS CAESAR

Echoing the reporter's sentiments, when the Rev. Frank Crane welcomed the general on behalf of the city, he represented, in eloquent fashion, the sentiments of most Americans. He likened William Booth to Julius Caesar, but pointed out the differences:

"One waded to fame through the blood of his enemies, the other conquered through the blood of the Lamb. One made war to rule men, the other makes war to serve them. One subdued kingdoms that he might exact tribute from them, the other approaches the kingdoms of the world having on his banner inscribed the legend, 'I seek not yours, but you.' In support of his sentiments, the whole audience stood and the air was white with the fluttering handkerchiefs of those who took this novel method of expressing their welcome to the distinguished visitor" (Ibid, Dec. 3). William Booth then spoke for two hours, "holding the attention of the audience to the very close of his address."

Chapter Ten

If the receptions accorded William Booth had thus far been beyond his expectations, when he traveled for the first time across the Great Divide and on to the Pacific Coast, he experienced an increase of adulation which was nearly indescribable.

In Denver, for example, which William Booth visited on December 9 and 10, he was lionized. He was not there, stated the *Rocky Mountain News*, for a "pleasure trip, saving souls is his business." It was a statement of which General Booth would heartily approve; for though the scenery was magnificent, and he had never seen the mountains or the mighty Colorado River, he was solely interested in lost souls. In fact, he would have approved of nearly everything that particular reporter had to say about him and the Salvation Army.

DISPLAY OF ARTISTRY

"Altogether, a remarkable lot of people are these Salvationists," continued the report. "They were seen at their very best yesterday, for the visit of their general had stirred all the religious enthusiasm of their natures. Poke bonnets sometimes enhance loveliness. Plain garb sometimes sets off beauty. Military coats often add materially to manly looks. So it came about that this Salvation Army of Colorado, as massed yesterday, proved a fine looking body. Its uniform is picturesque in a way. The flecks of red in bonnet and sash, cap and braid, give a touch of color quite artistic. The interest of the Army in its general was quite absorbing. Eyes were glistening and faces were aglow, until some of the sweet-faced lassies might have sat for a Raphaelite picture. Their volleys of 'Amens' came from the heart with such a ring that nerves were set tingling.

"Every Salvationist in Denver was in the great procession that marched from the two places of rendezvous. It was noisy, indeed, a boisterous crowd, and loud were the hallelujahs that rang out as the parade wended its way to the Coliseum. Red was the color that predominated, the women wearing badges of this color on dresses of blue, their heads adorned in the Quaker-like bonnet of darker color. The privates, who were gorgeous in red sweaters, were evidently proud of their distinctive costume, and as the string band played the notes of a hymn they responded with cries of 'Glory,' 'Glory to God,' 'Hallelujah,' 'Bless the Lord,' 'Bless His holy name.'

"The tambourine was gaily swung by the women, who sang as they marched, and added by words and gestures to the excitement which never lagged until the hush fell upon the great assemblage which was seated in the meeting place. The crowds that thronged the sidewalks along the lines of march were naturally attracted to this display, and men, women and children followed, anxious to see the remainder of the show. Those who were fortunate enough to obtain a seat in the already crowded hall found however, that there was something more to the gathering than a general hurrah."

THE LURE OF REVIVALS

What the reporter is alluding to, of course, and what reporters in the West seemed genuinely interested in, was William Booth's charisma as a revivalist. In most cities in the East, it was his public meetings—lectures about his *Darkest England* scheme—which garnered the most interest and acclaim. They were, indeed, for most Americans, the main attractions of his visits. And, for General Booth, they were the forums in which he could fulfill his main ambition, to make Americans aware of—and solicit their support for—the Army's social work.

For American Salvationists, however, though they attended every public meeting and enlivened them with their music and flag-waving, it was their general as spiritual leader and revivalist that they were most anxious to hear. It was William Booth's salvation and holiness meetings which touched their hearts and inspired them to greater service. And, in truth, though General Booth felt compelled to promote his *Darkest England* scheme, his great passion was still the salvation of souls. Even though more than half his meetings were mainly for the benefit of the public—crowded with local dignitaries, auxiliaries and local clergymen—he still cherished those moments (in his many officers councils and in his holiness and salvation meetings) when he could preach the gospel and deal with spiritual matters.

And it was those meetings which, for some reason, western reporters seemed most interested in. It was not that they paid no attention to William Booth's social plans, for it was clear to everyone that many of the vices which he talked about, and intended to deal with, were as prevalent in San Francisco as they were in London. They did indeed listen to him as he expounded on his "scheme" and they praised his ability to vivify the social degradation, which the Army was helping to alleviate. But they paid as much attention to, and described in as much detail, his preaching style and his salvation meetings.

Heartfelt Delivery

"The way General Booth works up an audience is marvelously artistic. At the outset he is disappointing. He starts rapidly, but often halts, hesitates and repeats in a tone inclined to nasal. But after a time he moves back from the pulpit. His voice gains strength and cleanness. He begins to move back and forth, up and down. Then, last night, in an instant, the whole character of the man seemed changed. He was a-quiver with excitement. His arms and his long index fingers swept through the air with startling rapidity. He was ablaze with earnestness. His age disappeared.

"His rapid movements kept pace with the torrent of words that fell from his lips. He talked right to hearts. He had his Army in tears. Then came his call to the repentant, quietly, sincerely, earnestly made. There was nothing studied, nothing theatrical. If ever a man spoke from the heart it was General Booth. As the speaker whom all had come to hear told in plain and tender words the story of the cross, old and young wept, and before the morning service closed, there knelt before the English general a band of contrite sinners" [*Denver Rocky Mountain News*, Dec. 10].

It was in the western newspapers, as well—the *Denver Rocky Mountain News*, the *Oakland Tribune*, the *San Francisco Morning Call*, the *Sacramento Daily Record-Union* and the *Los Angeles Times*—that we get a full sense of the distinctiveness and power of a Salvation Army meeting as conducted by General Booth. He would often, if it were a Sunday morning (and in no need of some socialite to introduce him), begin the meeting himself, wasting not a precious moment.

Down to Business

"Promptly at 10:30, the tall form of General Booth was seen making its way up one of the aisles leading to the platform. The great commander

was attired in a well-fitting suit of black, with a long-tailed coat reaching
to his knees, and carrying in his hand an odd-looking plug hat of the fashion of forty years ago. The general's coat was ornamented with big but-
tons and through its open front could be seen the bright red vest of the
Salvation Army. The general's gray hair and long gray beard gave him a
patriarchal appearance and his highly nervous manner indicated that he
was strung up to concert pitch for the heavy work of the day.

"There was no time lost in preliminaries. Walking straight to the
platform which he mounted with the agile step of a young man of 20, the
veteran warrior stepped to the front and said:

"'Everybody that is glad to see the general, say amen!'

"'Everybody bound to get a blessing, general or no general, say amen!'

"The responses came with redoubled force.

"'Now, have a good look at me and let's get down to business.'

"The general held the attention of his audience for five minutes as
he gradually unlimbered his guns . . . He said he had delivered 19 heavy
sermons in a week, 'heavy for me and heavy for my audiences,' but he
would attempt to do the talking and the people could do the singing.

THE MAIN THING

"'You don't have to know the tune in order to sing Salvation Army
songs,' said he. 'Just open your mouth and the tune sings itself.' The
audience laughed and the speaker remarked that salvation was the
main thing after all. There were two ways, he explained, to arrive at
salvation. One is through the brain, by reasoning and study, but it requires a long time and many people do not have brains enough to carry
them through on that line. The other plane solved the question by a
short cut. It simply consisted in 'feeling it out.' 'Amen, 'Amen,' shouted
300 lusty-lunged Salvationists" [*Denver Rocky Mountain News*, Dec.
10, 1894].

Having thus introduced himself, and the role he would play (that of
preaching the sermon), General Booth would then bring forward his "re-
serve forces." These were the officers who would lead the singing, sing
the solos, conduct the testimony period, and, most important, after the
sermon had been preached, lead people to the mercy seat. In his entourage were many local officers who could fulfill those tasks: Brigadier
French from St. Louis, for example, ranked high "as an exhorter and
could play any musical instrument ever made." But, most trusted and

capable—indeed, one of the best "platform men" the Salvation Army has ever known—was Colonel John Lawley, whom William Booth had brought with him from London for that very purpose.

An Alter Ego

Ostensibly, Lawley was General Booth's "general factotum" who, many days ahead of time, would check out the buildings in which he would be preaching and the homes at which he would be staying; who, on the nights of William Booth's "performances," would ensure that the doors were closed against possible latecomers (against any who might disrupt the general's train of thought), see that no windows allowed any light beams to blind his line of sight, and keep mothers with young babies from sitting in the front row.

But Lawley was much more than a factotum. He was an accomplished songwriter, excellent tenor and a brilliant speaker in his own right. And, by his very presence, he would impress his audience, for he was a barrel of a man with "a perfect jungle of red whiskers," who liked to assure his audiences that if God could save all of him, He could easily save any of them. He would start the meeting with a rousing Army song, "Come shout and sing, make heaven ring, with praises to our king," or by training the audience to sing a new chorus, "I do believe, I will believe, that Jesus died for me," repeating it over and over again until it stuck. And as the audience became enthused by the song, he would shout, "Everybody that's happy, say 'amen!'"

"Now think of your wives and children," the general would interject, "and let us have some serious chat. Let us pray—let us all pray. Major Malan will lead us. Now, major." And, after the prayer, Lawley would deepen the emotion caused by the fervency of the prayer by singing, "Life now will soon be waning, And evening bells will toll."

"Concluding the song [Lawley] uttered a short prayer, and again broke into song. It thrillingly described the sinner's fate when made to realize that the time for repentance had forever passed. Its force was multiplied when he engaged in an impassioned prayer, and from all sides came cries and murmurs of supplication.

Take all my sins away, take all my sins away;
O spotless Lamb, I come to thee;
Take all my sins away.

PRAYER AND BATTLE CRY

As the colonel sang, the words seemed as balm to wounded hearts . . .
While still on his knees he asked the audience to join in. "It will do you
good to sing," he urged. "Christ can take all the pretension out of your
heart."

"You should see, you should hear this man," a reporter later wrote.
"For only personal experience will convince you of his power. He's a
perfectly commonplace looking little man, with a heavy brown beard,
and the sweetest, the strongest of tenors. But his manner of conducting
a revival is the most delicately artistic, the most effective that one could
imagine. When the first words come from his lips you are not sure as to
whether he is singing or speaking, he half-intones the words of the
hymn, singing deliberately and enunciating with perfect clearness, and
the muffled notes of the cornet accompany him, no matter what the va-
garies he interpolates in his song, which is at once a prayer and a battle
cry. The music of the man's voice and the effect of his fervid eloquence
put a new meaning into stereotyped phrases. When he sings a verse of
an old hymn one wonders whether he has ever heard it before" [*San
Francisco Call*, March 1, 1898].

Thus urged by Lawley, the audience generally softly joined the refrain and the "prayer breathed forth in song in musical cadence tended
to make the scene solemnly dramatic. Emotion was in the air. As the
voices died away Colonel Lawley uttered a short but fervent prayer,
every sentence of which was pointed by ejaculations from all parts of
the hall, for mercy, for forgiveness and thankfulness . . . and when General Booth stood up to make his address the audience was apparently in
a receptive state of mind" [*Los Angeles Times*, Dec. 24, 1894].

For the next hour or so William Booth would preach, as most reporters called it, a "hot convicting" sermon—a sermon which, even by
late nineteenth-century standards, was quite literal in its interpretation
of Biblical truths and uncompromising in its insistence on living a sin-
free life dedicated to serving others.

SALVATION IS NOT . . .

"In defining what salvation to a man really is, what it really consists of,"
wrote the *Los Angeles Times*, William Booth "first explained at some

length what it is not. It is not merely making a profession of religion; and man cannot be saved without burning to declare the good news, but on the other hand the greatest humbugs are often the greatest professors. Nor is it a matter of feeling, albeit the saved one is filled with a feeling of deepest joy, but still it is possible to have such feeling and very little practical godliness. 'To be saved,' said the general in almost despairing accents, 'it means so much I can hardly dare touch it. It means a life of holiness, of goodness, following Jesus Christ, going into the world as Christ-men and Christ-women, and living a life of good and of sacrifice to others. It means a peaceful death and being borne on angels' wings.'

"To all present, the General urged, it meant all the sins of the past life being washed out; a perfect reconciliation with God. 'It seems too good to be true,' he added, 'but thank God it is true, for some of us have felt it in our own hearts. Those who have felt it cry out hallelujah.'

"A mighty thunder of hallelujahs went up through the roof.

Mighty River of Grace

"Earnestly appealing to sinners he recalled to them the vows made to mother or wife, or maybe to themselves while lying on a sick bed, of reforming their ways and meeting their loved ones on the other side. 'You say you have tried,' said he, 'that you meant to keep your vow, but you couldn't. Thank God there is a chance for you yet. Jesus Christ, the Deliverer, will save you from yourself. Now it's hard to do right, then it will be hard to do evil. Now it appears as if doing right is like climbing a steep hill, then going to heaven will seem like going down hill,' and the general tripped easily across the platform in illustration . . . 'The fact is,' and General Booth bent over with uplifted finger, 'you want the doctor but you don't want the physic [medicine], and that's what's the matter with you. But God can save to the utmost if you will let Him.'

"'Oh, men and women, I am talking to some of you, I know I am, who have had, so to speak, the romance of religion, for religion is the most romantic thing under heaven. How on your knees you have wept and vowed when you have thought of the dying world and the suffering of Christ, and said, 'My God, let me go!' You have come out at holiness meetings, knelt down and given God yourself, and your husband, and your children, and said, 'Lord, anywhere.' Then the first time your Lord has come and asked you to do something, which has had a cross in it—

you have shrunk back, saying, 'I cannot do it,' and gone on singing, 'Rescue the perishing,' and calling yourself a Christian. This cannot be. This must not be!

CALL TO ABUNDANT LIFE

"'Some people,' he cried, 'take their religion like they do their Worcester sauce—it's not their substantial food, it is just a flavor. Now, backslider, close your eyes and pray. I can say nothing more; it is for you to act. Now kneel down, bow your heads and pray.'

"Colonel Lawley stood up. 'Ask them straight, colonel,' said the general. 'It's salvation or damnation tonight. We'll never see many of them again, till we meet them at the judgment seat'" [Ibid, Dec. 24, 1894].

Most often, then, it was Lawley who did the final entreating, calling upon sinners to come forward and repent. And sometimes, when a chorus had ended, or Lawley had stopped pleading for a minute, the general, on his knees, would break in again: "Oh, that I could hear some soul say tonight, I repent. Oh, that some of these newspapermen here would say it. They think they are not sinners, but they are." And the battle for souls would continue until both Lawley and General Booth were satisfied that they had said all they could say, prayed all they could pray, and had exhausted all powers of persuasion. And then the meeting ended in a glorious song of victory.

Chapter Eleven

The train ride from Colorado Springs to Salt Lake City covered some 700 miles and took 26 hours to accomplish; from Salt Lake City, after an overnight stay and a meeting in the Tabernacle, it was another 800 miles and a 36 hour ride into Oakland, California.

It was, by any stretch of the imagination, a tiring affair. For William Booth, however, it was time to catch up on his correspondence and recover from a nasty cold. For his entourage, it was a chance to enjoy the scenic delights. "We never went out of our way," wrote Major Taylor, the English *War Cry* correspondent, "to see wonders or curiosities of nature; we were much too animated with the spirit of our general [a polite way of saying William Booth did not encourage it] to give much thought to anything but the same objects to which he showed such unstinted devotion. However, God placed some of His handiwork before our very eyes, that we shall never forget. Such, for instance, as the sights we saw in crossing the Rocky Mountains. One or two of us had never seen a real mountain till we saw Pike's Peak. The effect upon us was not only a surprise, but it produced praise.

PEAKS OF INSPIRATION

"Especially were we amazed—overcome—in the passage of the Royal Gorge, Colorado. Colonel Lawley, Major Halpin and I squeezed ourselves out on to the steps of the rear car, where, amid almost blinding coal-dust and a roar as of thunder we hung on as our train threaded the wonderful canyon. Other mountains that struck us very much later on were Mount Tacoma, Mount Shasta, and Mount Baker, all beautiful peaks, covered with snow. These gave joy and inspiration to our souls" [*All the World*].

As did the "hallelujah" times which followed. For though the schedule was a demanding one, the blessings were abundant.

WEST COAST FERVOR

In San Francisco General Booth's salvation meetings were again typical of most. The Salvationists themselves, from all over the States, were wildly enthusiastic. "Of course they were," wrote a reporter for the *San Francisco Call*. "They couldn't be Salvationists if they weren't—that's what the general said and he really ought to know all about it."

"'Stir 'em up! Stir 'em up!' exclaimed the general as the clarion-voiced Lawley gave out another hymn, and Lawley did. He sang at them and with them, and higher and louder than any of them, and they shouted and sang at him again and again. They cried 'Amen,' they 'fixed bayonets,' they 'fired volleys' and did all manner of the things in such cases provided by the Salvation Army regulations. Some people might have called the pandemonium they made enthusiasm. It wasn't. It was religious fervor of the most vivid sort and had a staying power.

"The occasion being his last opportunity of addressing San Franciscans, for some time, anyhow, the general was very earnest and very dramatic. He wrought himself to perfect frenzies in his earnestness to touch the, as yet, unregenerate; he waved his arms and shook his fists, thrust his trembling fingers in his hoary locks and jumped around the platform like one thoroughly aroused to the peril he depicted in the climaxes to be brought about. It was really a grand sight to see such a patriarch, by his own confession on the brink of the grave and welcoming death, calling upon the sinning to leave their ways and cling to Jehovah."

JOSHUA'S OATH

"The great audience was more completely under his spell than it had ever been before. Women wept, and men—not Salvationists, either—as they hung awestruck on his almost inspired utterances. He absolutely seemed to rise out of the enfeebled form and to tower aloft, a veritable pillar of strength.

"'It is very, very possible,' he said, sorrowfully, 'that this may be the last time I may speak to you in this world. I shall be very glad, if God spares my life and you invite me to come back to San Francisco. If you invite me to come back again I shall come back if I live—I shall come back again, if I live, whether you invite me or not.'

"And the general chuckled cheerily at the little joke in the last few words and the crowd cheered as loudly as it did the first time it set eyes on him . . .

"[O]ne of the things he wished to impress upon his hearers before he left San Francisco, maybe for the last time, was that every one of them should say like Joshua, 'As for me and my house, we will serve the Lord.'

"'Like Joshua, I can remember the day, some fifty years ago, in a little town in England (I think I can remember the hour and the moon as it shone over me), I committed myself to Jehovah. That hour has passed, but that resolution has never changed. I want all of you to do like Joshua—stand fast, committing yourselves to Jehovah and nailing his colors to the mast. I don't want anybody to do anything tonight who doesn't know what he is doing.'

ANGELS AND SAINTS

"He pictured to that audience the beauties of that independence of spirit which came to those who served the Lord, and the relative influence it had in deciding others. He pictured the solicitation of mothers for the salvation of their souls, and said he believed their spirits when departed hovered about and around, striving to guide the dear ones left and right.

"'I believe most emphatically in the ministering of angels and saints.'

"He concluded: 'I come to my closing proposition tonight. Nobody in this house can tell to what extent his decision tonight for Jesus Christ is going to affect the decision of a crowd of other people.'

"He repeated this several times, the more earnestly each time, as if to impress upon his hearers the words, and then he called upon those who wished to decide to come to the mercy-seat. There were many responses, and the meeting continued for half an hour, amid much singing and rejoicing" [Dec. 20, 1894].

LOS ANGELES

In Los Angeles, in an atmosphere "that seemed to breathe Paradise," William Booth was at his feistiest best. With soldiers numbering 1,000 present from the whole Southern California Division—from San Diego, San Bernadino, Redlands, Riverside, Pomona, Pasadena, El Monte, Ventura, Santa Barbara, San Luis Obispo, Santa Monica and Phoenix, Arizona—he thanked them for their welcome but reprimanded them (kindly he thought) for not praying and singing as they ought. "You Salvationists," he told them, "are a lazy lot; you look on while we're singing. What's the matter with you? You look like muscular fellows [he was now looking at the soldiers on the platform], so open your mouths and sing, or come down off your perch and let others get up there." He was smiling as he said it, but he meant it.

And in the same forthright manner, he laid on them the demanding responsibility of being Salvationists. To be saved, he said, (in almost despairing accents) "means so much I hardly dare touch it. It means a life of holiness, of goodness, following Jesus Christ, going into the world as Christ-men and Christ-women, and living a life of sacrifice for others." It was obviously a disappointment to him that most people, even Salvationists, were not living up to this ideal, especially the life of service.

TAKING A TALLY

"How many soldiers here," he asked, "if angels were to come down and ask you what you have done during the year, how many souls you had saved, could make reply? Have you saved one soul?" he persisted. He paused a moment and then inquired: "Well, what keeps your mouths shut?" Continuing in impassioned voice, he said: "In a few moments hundreds of professing Christians in this house will show that they have neither the courage nor the ability to ask their neighbor, sitting next to them, if he or she is saved. A whole lot of you have just enough religion to make you miserable, that's all. You are not enjoying the sweets of the world, nor the sweetness of the Kingdom of God" [*Los Angeles Times*, Dec. 24, 1894].

Earnestly appealing, he called them to their true mission. "The general having thus pointed out the way of salvation made the usual request that all bend in silent prayer, while Colonel Lawley continued the exhortation. For some time he pleaded and exhorted in vain and then occurred a most touching incident. An elderly lady came forward from the side aisle and sank on her knees in penitence. A young Salvation lassie bent down and put her arms around her, while a tall, bronzed soldier knelt on the other side and whispered in the woman's ear. The soldier six months ago figured in far different scenes.

"At that time, and for 20 years previous, more or less, Alf Oakley was known throughout Southern California as a pretty hard character, and a saloon-keeper at San Bernadino. As a short-card man and general manipulator of the pasteboards he was known to be an expert, but he joined the Army and became a changed man. Yesterday, he it was who whispered words of peace and hope in the ear of his mother, who, like him, has found refuge through the instrumentality of the Salvation Army" [Ibid].

CHRISTMAS PUDDING

On Christmas Day, 1894, William Booth boarded a train for Sacramento. "Christmas fare was not, however, altogether absent. We stopped at mid-day at a wayside depot, where we got turkey and cranberry sauce, and what was poetically described as 'plum pudding.' We charitably assumed that the cook had never seen the real article, but had made the preparation from a description at about third-hand of somebody who had enjoyed that privilege" [*All the World*].

In Sacramento, the local Army corps had an unusual Christmas Day, marching to the train depot with the Charioteers' Band from San Francisco, and back to the Congregational Church where their general lectured on his *Darkest England* scheme. On the following evening he talked of the Army's progress throughout the world. "The Army," he told an overflow audience, "preached a religion of gladness and joy and hope and cheerfulness. There was nothing in it of somber and depressing character. For the method of the Army he had no apology to make. It serves its purpose, it attains the end—the salvation and uplifting of men and women and the sanctification of their lives. To do good, to help, to cheer, to make clean, to teach the gospel of cleanliness, simplicity, cheerfulness and hope, that is the mission of the Army" [*Sacramento Daily Record-Union*, Dec. 27].

WATCH NIGHT IN SEATTLE

From there it was on to Portland, Tacoma and Seattle. In the last of these cities there were, so said the *War Cry* correspondent, 20,000 people on the street to welcome the general on his arrival, and in the city square he had an audience of 10,000 cheering citizens. A civic arch had been erected of evergreens, bearing the motto in electric lights: "Welcome, Booth!" It was here that William Booth saw the old year out and 1895 ushered in. It was suggested that the general, almost dropping from fatigue and exhaustion, would not participate in the watch-night service, but when the time came he would not hear of it. He again "spoke words of loving entreaty that the year about to dawn should be wholly and solely devoted to the service of God. When he had finished he sunk upon his knees, leaning against a chair, and would not leave the building till the New Year had arrived and brought with it to the altar a line of penitents."

It seemed, stated Colonel Lawley, that God Himself wished General Booth to have an everlasting good impression of the United States by having him finish this part of his tour among the "happiest, most Blood-and-Fire comrades that can be found in this or in any other part of the world. To say the least, these Northern Pacific Salvationists went wild with delight. They were too happy to keep on their feet, and they literally danced and jumped for joy." William Booth was filled with optimism at the thought of what the future could be for such enthusiasts.

Chapter Twelve

Returning to the eastern cities—Buffalo, Boston, Worcester, Providence, Springfield and New York—after he had taken a month-long detour through Canada, William Booth was, as on his initial visits, given magnanimous receptions.

In Buffalo, on February 15, 1895, after spending Friday morning and afternoon in council with his officers and soldiers, the general was received with overwhelming enthusiasm at the spacious Music Hall by 3,700 people. There were, say the reports, more than 135 leading citizens in attendance—bishops, senators, generals, ministers, doctors and lawyers—quite a few of whom occupied places on the platform. "Mr. H.D. Blakeslee, one of Buffalo's sterling citizens, introduced the general, who touched to tears the vast assemblage by his simple, earnest recital of the needs and woes of the classes in whose interest this tour was largely undertaken. A liberal collection was taken" [*All the World*].

"On our way to Boston," writes Major Taylor, "we got a foretaste of the things in store for us. Vast crowds of people had assembled at the depots at Pittsfield and Worcester, to whom the general addressed a few affectionate words."

EXCITEMENT IN BOSTON

In Boston the renowned Faneuil Hall, gracing the city since 1742, was placed at William Booth's disposal for a welcome meeting where he was introduced to the more than 2,000 Bostonians who had turned out to hear him. He was introduced on that occasion by the noted theologian and preacher, Dr. Joseph Cook, who would, on Monday, give a public lecture—the 244th lecture in his famous series of Boston Monday Lectures—on the Salvation Army. On the Sunday preceding that lecture,

William Booth conducted three meetings in the Mechanics Institute, a building capable of accommodating from five to eight thousand people (depending on whom you read).

"For an hour before the time of the service," stated the *Zion's Herald* (Feb. 20); "crowds were at the door, filling the sidewalk and street in front. A half hour before beginning the service the hall was well filled and the members of the Army occupied the time in song and prayer. No moment was allowed to run to waste, and in all these preliminary services there was a marked intensity and enthusiasm. They sang lustily and prayed with great power.

A POWERHOUSE

"The general, on entering the hall, was received with cheers and a shout. He bowed in recognition, and at once assumed control of the services. He held the audience with a cunning hand. He opened by reading a hymn, with brief and pithy comments on the sentiment. In this sort of running commentary, he is extremely happy, making points and touching them so lightly as never to be tedious. He followed it up in reading the Scripture out of which his text came, making parts of the chapter to blaze out with new and unexpected light.

"We are often told that men have ceased to be interested in the gospel; but here is a man who knows how to speak pertinently and obtains the ear of the largest audience. The man himself is a power; he acts as an electric battery in the midst of a great audience. He has the intellectual qualities of both the statesman and the boss. He grasps the subject in its wide relations and is equally at home in details. His forces are intellectual as well as moral; his sermons are full of burning points; he has wit which flashes out in many of his expressions, and a pathos which occasionally melts the heart."

The *Boston Daily Advertiser* more graphically reported that "General Booth threw back his long coat; he placed his hands now on his hips, now on the armholes of his scarlet jersey; his eyeglasses dangling from their cord swung around and out, reflecting the light; he gesticulated with both arms, sometimes raising them high above his head, or sweeping before him great waves of metaphorical sin; often he stamped; and sometimes he knelt.

PATHS TO PERDITION

"'Where will you be,' he exclaimed, 'when Boston and everything else that is pleasant and everything else that charms you has passed away? You can go to hell without being a liar or a thief or a wicked man at all. There are very dirty roads that lead to hell, and there are some that look very clean. I don't know what you are, or who you are, or where you go to church, or what your belief is, if your life isn't right with God, then you are bound for hell. There are people who say the belief in the devil is growing weaker and weaker, in fact it's almost disappeared, but I tell you the devil laughs to himself and cries, '*Aha, aha!* How easy it is to deceive these fools!'"

On that Sunday the *Daily Advertiser* estimated that as many as 25,000 people filled the Mechanics Institute for the three revival meetings. "We admired the faith of Brigadier Brewer [the divisional commander] in securing a building that would accommodate nearly 10,000 people," wrote the *War Cry* correspondent, "and we appreciated the work that must [have been done] to fill it to overflowing, leaving thousands out on the sidewalk."

BEHIND THE SCENES

Much of the credit for having done so should have gone to the energetic Edward Justus Parker, who was then general-secretary for the division. In his autobiography, *My Fifty-Eight Years* (1943), he gives us an insight into the kind of work that went into the preparations for William Booth's visit—preparatory work that was carried out all across America by other devoted officers as well. He says: "I recall clearly that on this occasion there were some misgivings about the possibility of securing audiences large enough to fill the huge Mechanics Building, which seated 10,000 people. Skeptics reminded us that Bostonians invariably went to church on the Sabbath.

"Nevertheless, the Mechanics Building was secured, and the founder had an audience of 8,000 persons on Sunday morning and 10,000 on Sunday night. How was this feat accomplished? By announcing these meetings everywhere, through the medium of both press and pulpit. Moreover, for several days preceding the event, posters carrying the bold letters, 'SUNDAY NEXT, GENERAL BOOTH DAY,' covered the front of all of the trolley cars in the city. I recall, too, that in addition to the Sunday triumph, 2,000 people paid a $1.00 admission charge to hear the founder lecture at the Academy of Music on Monday evening. There was also a further meeting, attended by approximately 300 preachers at Park Street Church. (The press said 500—oh, generous press!)

"In addressing these ministers the founder, as always, spoke from his heart, avoiding theological discussion and controversy. Often he would introduce passages which were of the character of testimony to his own experience of enjoyment of God's grace, guidance and blessing" [pp. 119-121]. During William Booth's visit, while most Salvationists were enjoying their general's "words of wisdom," Parker (and other officers like him in other cities) was "scurrying hither and yon," making certain that everything went as planned. Without such unstinting groundwork General Booth's tour could not have been the success that it was.

JOSEPH COOK'S LECTURE

Another highlight of General Booth's visit to Boston was Dr. Joseph Cook's 244th Boston Monday Lecture. A tradition for many years, at which the elite of Boston's intellectual community was nearly always present, the lecture was held at Cook's Park Street Church, known as the "church of firsts" ("My Country 'Tis of Thee" was first sung there in 1831). To an overflow audience of "preachers, teachers, students and other educated men" (many were standing in the aisles on the floor and in the galleries; window sills were occupied as seats), Dr. Cook gave his first public lecture on William Booth and the Salvation Army. No doubt adding to the interest was the fact that General Booth himself gave a 30-minute overview of the Army's work (frequently interrupted by applause) before Dr. Cook lectured (see Appendix A).

A GLOWING TRIBUTE

Dr. Cook was nothing if not gracious and complimentary. Of William Booth's work he stated:

"The Army wishes to be above all suspicion of being a money-making machine. It does ask for contributions from all his audiences. It does call for self-denial on the part of its officers; and this is practiced heroically by both the men and women. It has received large sums of money from many sources but is immensely above all suspicion of seeking loaves and fishes for any other purpose than to feed the hungry and perishing."

And of William Booth himself, whom he had witnessed in action, he stated (and later wrote):

"His power as an orator is in his sympathy with the poor, his manly simplicity and courage, his frequent flashes of wit and humor, his rugged alert and piercing common-sense. All these elements are suffused in his case with the most unmistakably genuine religious awe, self-consecration, and self-forgetfulness. He speaks always with the full force of his human faculties and gives to a careful observer the impression that he is not without divine assistance. His soul is of a lofty and intense type, Hebraic rather than Greek or Roman in structure, not given to philosophical speculation or to flights of imagination, but keenly sagacious along all the lines of practical effort to bring men into a religious life.

"He appeals to the will, and everywhere he arouses his hearers to the duty of immediate self-surrender to the Holy Spirit which, in his best moments, seems to pervade the whole impression received by the assembly" [*Our Day* (Sept. 1895): 119-24.] It was a sincere tribute from one great Christian leader to another, and no doubt contributed greatly to William Booth's prestige in the city of Boston and, when reported, throughout the whole country.

COLLEGE STUDENTS APPLAUD

By the end of February 1895, William Booth's tour of America was almost over. There remained but a few engagements, the most pleasant of which was a lecture to the students of Harvard University. General Booth thoroughly enjoyed talking to young people who, in turn, enjoyed his frankness and humor. He had done so with great success at the University of Chicago and now, here at Harvard, 1,500 of its 3,000 students came to hear him speak, applauding and cheering throughout his address and finally escorting him to the university's gates with "shouts of goodwill ringing in his ears." And, finally, after putting in appearances at Springfield and Providence, William Booth led two great meetings in New York, the first at the Cooper Union on February 25th and the last at Carnegie Music Hall on the 26th.

PRAGMATIC AND PERSONAL

"It is doubtful," wrote the *War Cry* correspondent, "whether any audience throughout the trip was more enthusiastic in its sympathetic admiration of himself and his schemes than that which filled the Carnegie Music Hall on the evening before his departure. After expressing his appreciation for the kindness and sympathy that had been accorded him from one end of the country to the other, he proceeded to set forth very plainly the practical character of the salvation possessed by the Army, and to make very powerful personal application to all present. After promising that all branches of the *Darkest England* scheme should be established in the United States, and that in the future he would, if possible, pay an annual visit to this country, he concluded with a heart-stirring appeal to all to fight faithfully for God and meet him in heaven."

"Rarely," wrote a *New York Tribune* reporter, "has the handsome hall at Fifty-Seventh Street held so large a crowd or been the scene of such continuous enthusiasm as was witnessed last evening. A noteworthy feature of the assembly was the beautiful costumes of the women and the high social standing in general of the people who occupied the boxes of the first circle. The attention with which the general was listened to, and the flattering applause with which he was frequently interrupted, should send him away with the belief that the American people recognize, beyond the shadow of a doubt, that the methods of the Salvation Army have borne good and commendable results, especially among that class of people its leaders try hardest to reach" (Feb. 27).

At his departure next day (February 27), as he was about to board the American steamship Paris, the national staff band which had been playing such inspiring tunes as "The Crowning Day is Coming" and "Victory for Me" began "Auld Lang Syne" and kept it up until "the ship floated out into the river and was carried away upstream." Then, as she passed down again, "the brass instruments sounded out 'Home, Sweet Home!' And as the record-making racer steamed past, a handkerchief fluttered from the deck." William Booth was on his way home.

Mission Accomplished

Judging by all of the available evidence, one can say that the 1894-95 tour of America was, in terms of public acceptance of the Army, an outstanding success. It was exhausting. The whole tour, through Canada and the United States, which included stops (from one to three days) in some 81 cities required rough travel which covered almost 19,000 miles (847 hours aboard trains). William Booth addressed some 437,000 people in more than 340 sermons and speeches (47 short and 293 longer than an hour), gave 180 interviews, attended more than a hundred "special engagements" (meetings with influential people, banquets and such things as a speech to the students at Harvard), and devoted 430 hours to business.

Today, when we watch a presidential candidate criss-cross this vast nation, speaking daily to immense audiences, we often marvel at the stamina, the sheer will power, required to do so. How much more do we marvel at that of William Booth, in an age when travel was not by fast jet but by often slow trains, subject to weather-determined schedules, sleeping in strange beds every night, eating foods he could not often tolerate (suffering as he was constantly with dyspepsia), and having to speak twice daily whether he felt like it or not. He was not, we might add, a young man like United States President Barak Obama, but a 65-year-old man, on the verge of what normally would have been a well-earned retirement.

Generous Outreach

But it was profitable and pleasant. General Booth's plans for an extended social outreach were received by Americans with great generosity. Though we cannot be certain just how much money was raised, it can be estimated, based on individual cities, that more than $200,000 went into Salvation Army coffers. The incentive to establish new social services, and increase those already in existence in American cities, was considerably enhanced by the moral support rendered by local auxiliary groups.

As for the evangelical side of the Army's work, it too was raised considerably in the public's estimation, for it became quite clear that this was not a renegade sect, but a middle-of-the-road revival organization very much in the Wesleyan tradition. Clearly, William Booth's sermons, as well as his public lectures, had met with nationwide approval. Not only were his eloquence and personal charm quite captivating, but his message struck a chord in the hearts of ordinary Americans. Assuredly, from a public point of view, the 1894-95 tour had been a success.

FAMILY DISPUTE

Privately, however, there were clouds on the horizon. What was unknown to the public (and to most Salvationists), and only known to a few of the hierarchy, was that relations between father and son—between William and Ballington—had become very strained during the trip. The father, as general, was concerned that the Army was becoming just a little too Americanized—that the American flag at most public functions took precedence over the "yellow, red and blue"; that a spirit of autonomy, along with a dissatisfaction with English rule, was beginning to pervade the American troops. The son chafed under his father's dictatorial attitude, feeling he was neither being consulted nor given credit for the work he was doing.

THE SHADOW OF SECESSION

Could it have been noticed, when the steamship Paris pulled away from New York harbor on February 27, that Ballington's farewell wave did not seem nearly as affectionate as one might think it should have been? Perhaps not. But, in fact, a rift had developed between father and son early in the tour, had widened considerably as the tour had proceeded and, though neither father or son could foresee any sort of major separation of power, within a year one would occur. A split within the American ranks would again cause many Salvationists to secede and would lead to the creation of yet another rival organization called The Volunteers of America. When William Booth made his third visit to America in 1898 it was again out of necessity—to repair the damage done by the defection of Ballington and Maud Booth in 1896.

Visit 3: 1898

Supporting a New Regime

The Salvation Army is by the very principles of its order an autocracy. Its commander-in-chief is an absolute despot, though he may be a consecrated, conscientious, and benevolent despot. In our time, and certainly in our country, such despotism can be maintained only in case he who possesses the authority exercises such discretion in wielding it as to allow large liberty to departmental and other subordinate heads. Local self-government is inherent in American institutions . . . General Booth has not been wise enough to perceive the necessity of such flexibility, and therefore his organization has suffered fracture.

The [New York] Outlook, March 7, 1896

1898 Itinerary

Arrived at New York on the S.S. St. Paul Jan. 15

Meeting with Ballington Jan. 16

To Canada Jan. 17-Feb. 7

Washington, DC: meeting with President McKinley Feb. 10-11

Pittsburgh, Pa. Feb. 12-14

Columbus, Ohio. Feb. 15

Cincinnati, Ohio Feb. 16-17

St. Louis, Mo. Feb. 18

Kansas City, Mo. Feb. 19-20

Denver, Co. Feb. 22

Los Angeles, Ca. Feb. 25

Oakland, Ca. Feb. 26-27

San Francisco, Ca. Feb. 28-March 3

Portland, Ore. March 5-6

Seattle, Wash. March 7

Victoria and Vancouver, Canada March 8-9

Spokane, Wash. March 11-13

Snowbound travel to Winnipeg, March 14-15

Grand Forks, S.D. (unexpected stop) Mar. 16

Winnipeg, Canada Mar. 17

Minneapolis, Minn. Mar. 19-21

St. Paul, Minn. March 22

Milwaukee, Wis. March 23

Red Jacket, Mich. March 24

Ishpeming, Mich. March 25

Chicago, Ill. March 26-31

Indianapolis, Ind. April 1

Cleveland, Ohio April 2-3

Detroit, Mich. April 4

Rochester, NY. April 6

Boston/Cambridge, Mass. April 9-11

Philadelphia, Pa. April 12-13

Troy, NY. April 15

Buffalo, NY. April 17

New York City April 19-26

Sailed for Liverpool, April 27

Chapter Thirteen

When William Booth left New York on February 27, 1895, at the end of his second tour of America, it was with some anxiety about the future of the American wing of his Salvation Army. Though his visit, aimed primarily at promoting his *Darkest England* scheme, had been eminently successful, a rift between Ballington and himself had occurred—a divergence of opinion regarding autocracy and the oppressive nature of rules and regulations—which caused him both personal anguish and concern for the stability of the Army.

There is, of course, no reason to believe that General Booth foresaw the near-disastrous result of this difference of opinion; nor did he expect that when he next returned to America he would again, as in 1886, be helping to rescue the Army from the unhappy effects of rebellion—trying to restore soldierly morale, and trying to repair a severe loss of public support, but such was the case.

SHAKEN TO THE CORE

For, less than a year after that second visit, Ballington and Maud Booth had not only resigned from the Army, but had established a rival religious organization which they called The Volunteers of America. They had, in the process, influenced a large number of officers and soldiers to leave the Army, had considerably weakened the support of the Army's Auxiliary League (as many as 4,000 wealthy patrons had supported its work), and had caused a noticeable decline in public sympathy. The Army was, as one historian put it, "shaken to its foundation" and it took a great deal of ingenuity and personal influence on the part of both William Booth and the new commanders, Frederick and Emma Booth-Tucker, to restore it to its former position of respect.

STRIFE PERSISTS

The Booth-Tuckers, appointed in April 1896, had in fact taken the Army a long way on the road to recovery. They had done so by instituting a vigorous program of social work, by affecting a centralized control of the Army's finances, and by courting other influential Americans (mainly Emma's task) to help replenish the Auxiliary League. In spite of their valiant efforts, however, and even though membership was increasing (in satisfying if not dramatic numbers), there was still much turmoil in the ranks.

The exact relationship between the evangelical and social wings was not yet clear to many officers, and the obvious return to an English-controlled system rankled many others. William's visit, in February and March of 1898, would, it was felt, do much to quell their fears and bring stability to the organization. It would also convince Americans of his integrity and do much to promote the new social initiatives begun by Frederick and Emma.

Before that effort could be undertaken, however, and to give the general a respite from such public pressure as he had just undergone, it was decided that the first leg of his tour (January 18 to February 7) would be through eastern Canada. By the time he returned, it was reasoned, the "Ballington Booth issue" might have receded from the public's mind. In this assumption the tour's organizers were correct. When William Booth returned to the United States on February 10, and until the end of his tour on April 27, the matter of reconciliation was hardly ever raised.

DEAR BRAMWELL

"I feel sure," he wrote to his son, Bramwell, that "every trace" of the Ballington affair (and the "slanderous campaign" he had waged), "will be swept away" and that "however dissatisfied a few creatures may feel, our own people will be so enthused and carried away, that I shall leave them enthusiastically confident and determined to [be] the Salvation Army. That is the burden of my exhortations everywhere—that is what they have to learn."

Chapter Fourteen

When William Booth began the United States portion of his 1898 American tour he did so in dramatic fashion—in a manner calculated to gain the attention of the American public and give American Salvationists a reason to stand tall. At noon on February 10, he officiated as honorary chaplain to the United States Senate and offered prayer at the opening of its session.

HISTORIC MOMENT

"He invoked the divine blessing upon the Senate and its members," wrote the *New York Times*, "and besought the Great Ruler of All to continue His favor to those here gathered for the ruling and regulating of this great and mighty nation, and that all that might here be done be to the honor and glory of God. He prayed that this country might move forward in the march of Christianity so that it might be an example to all other nations on earth. Mr. and Mrs. Booth-Tucker, the son-in-law and daughter of General Booth, were in the gallery during the prayer."

"The scene," exclaimed the *War Cry* reporter, "was one which will live forever. To us of the general's retinue it appeared as if the cluster of rich associations which cling round the historic edifice was receiving an important addition—that although history could not be said by any means to be repeating itself, yet the mind somehow or other traveled rapidly and easily back and forth between George Washington and William Booth, and a link was found to exist which brings the two upon common ground. They are each the father of a new nation—the one political, the other spiritual."

MEETING WITH MCKINLEY

More prestigious, perhaps, and certainly as influential in terms of public esteem, was the fact that at 3 p.m. the same afternoon, General

Booth and Commander Booth-Tucker were granted an audience with President William McKinley. They talked of many things, but most especially of the Army's new social initiatives, and William Booth was surprised, but very pleased, to learn just how familiar President McKinley was with the Army's work. "The president received his callers very cordially," stated the *New York Times*, "and in the course of an interview, which lasted about 15 minutes, expressed to General Booth his great admiration for him and for the great work of the Salvation Army, especially in the United States" [*New York Times*, Feb. 10, 1898].

That President McKinley—and indeed most of the senators—admired the Salvation Army did not stem entirely from a respect for General Booth. It had as much to do with the efforts of Frederick and Emma Booth-Tucker in shaping a new vision for the organization. They had, in fact, begun to steer the Army in America in a new direction by reemphasizing and intensifying its social outreach. By the time Booth-Tucker's term as commander was over (Emma died in a railway crash in 1903 and Frederick left America in 1904), the Salvation Army in America was resolutely on its way to becoming one of America's foremost social service agencies.

BOOTH-TUCKER CAMPAIGN

In 1898, at the time of William Booth's visit, that transformation was well under way. "The Booth-Tuckers," writes Salvation Army historian Edward McKinley, "arrived in America dazzled by the golden future that surely lay before the Army in such a prosperous and energetic country—once the Army's activities were properly organized. There would be little time, and less inclination, to linger over unhappy memories if the great work of the Army was pushed forward with sufficient vigor.

"To Booth-Tucker the blueprint for that campaign was already at hand—*In Darkest England*—which he regarded not merely as a general guideline but as an inspiration, the final revelation on social questions. And what was more certain to draw the support of the public and the loyalty of the wavering auxiliaries back to the Salvation Army than a large-scale advance in the social campaign? All was clear to Booth-Tucker: there could be no delay" [*Somebody's Brother* (1986: 31-32)].

Expansion of Social Work

In a very short time, then, Booth-Tucker was announcing new rescue homes, shelters, food depots, prison-gate homes, homes for "waifs and strays" and labor bureaus. The "feed-the-poor at Christmas" program was begun and more than 25,000 were fed in New York alone. The American public was confronted by the ubiquitous Christmas kettle, while Salvationists and auxiliaries were encouraged to support the effort by placing pennies in their "mercy boxes." And they were rewarded with frequent news of the openings of new workingmen's hotels, salvage brigades, second-hand stores, industrial homes, and other social institutions— "springing up all around us as if at the touch of a magician's wand," stated the *War Cry* [Feb. 1897]. In his 1898 report, entitled "The Social Work in the United States," Booth-Tucker reported that in just that year the number of social institutions in America had increased from 28 to 85.

Two Farm Colonies

The most ambitious project of all, however—the one beginning to become a reality during William Booth's visit and the one that gained the support of such high-placed officials as President McKinley—was the Farm Colony. Booth-Tucker's aim in creating "social farms" was to bring together the "landless man and the manless land." He stated it succinctly in these words: "Place the waste labor on the waste land, by means of waste capital, and thereby convert this modern trinity of waste into a unity of production."

Booth-Tucker's "farm colonies" were not, as William Booth had envisioned, a means of transporting people from England to the New World (though that might be what British countries like Canada would agree to), but were purely a national venture which would move the "surplus and unfortunate population from [American] cities to land that was capable of being irrigated and then farmed." In August, 1897 the first such farm was established at Fort Romie, near Soledad, California. The second, to be opened later in 1898, at Fort Amity in eastern Colorado, was already being advertised and prepared for occupation by "selected" pioneers.

The land, purchased at about $25 an acre by the Army, was not given away to the prospective farmers, but lent on credit for a period of

ten years by which time, it was thought, they would have paid for the
farms and perhaps have also earned enough to live on. "May these
happy and wholesome farm colonies be multiplied by the thousand,"
wrote one enthusiastic supporter, "and may they take hundreds of thousands of unfortunate town dwellers to the busy but serene and wholesome life of the irrigated farm!" That was Booth-Tucker's intention, and
the visit of his father-in-law, the man who had first expounded the idea
and whose reputation alone would attract nationwide support, was an
opportune moment to push the project to its fullest potential.

VOICING CONFIDENCE

Therefore, in most of William Booth's public lectures throughout this
visit, he not only told of the Army's rescue and rehabilitative work in
Great Britain, but was able to make specific reference to the work being done in America. The farms—two now a certainty and another in the
planning stage—would give men a chance to "earn a place for [them-
selves] in the world, and the scheme can be improved upon and broad-
ened from time to time as experience warrants." About $100,000 was
needed to give the scheme a start, and of this amount about $45,000 had
already been raised. He was confident of its success; as he also was of
the Booth-Tuckers' newest venture—"salvage" work.

SALVAGING CITY WASTE

This new plan for recycling city waste had just been adopted in Chicago
and New York. The scheme would not only provide temporary work for
needy men, but be a means of "permanent elevation of the men by the
Army's spiritual work and association." As the population of the United
States increased, so did the extremes of affluence and poverty. The Salvation Army was, General Booth said, well organized to meet the effects
of such disparity, and the lives of poor Americans were improving as a
result of its efforts.

That was the theme of William Booth's many lectures and it was one
which, even if some thought it somewhat self-congratulatory, most
Americans did not mind hearing over and over. For, even though many

had heard him just four years earlier, preaching the same gospel message and describing, in his inimitable style, the progress of both the Army and its social work, they again flocked to his meetings, attended his press conferences, and sought his advice just as avidly as before. And almost everywhere he went, to most of the same cities as in 1894, newspaper editors graciously acknowledged his presence.

SHIFT IN PUBLIC OPINION

"Time was, and not so very long ago, when the term 'Salvation Army' was a synonym of noise and nuisance; of low-grade evangelistic effort and blatant unreason; of gutter gospel masquerading in ridiculous uniform. The welcome accorded to General Booth upon his arrival in Portland yesterday, and the consideration that is being shown him and his associates by churches as a body, and by people as individuals, tell of the change in public opinion in regard to the work of this body.

"True, there are many people who see and acknowledge the power which the organization has been for good, who do not, nevertheless, endorse many of the means by which its ends are reached, but it is true also that in helping those who of all others are most in need of moral uplifting, the methods discountenanced have been greatly successful. The balance-sheet between tolerance and intolerance has been rendered, and by its showing the good which has been done by the Salvation Army is found to offset the objectionable methods through which it has been wrought" [*Morning Oregonian*, March 6, 1898].

FASCINATION

What reporters found fascinating and took great delight in describing was William Booth's physical appearance and his preaching style. They loved his sense of drama, his vivid depictions of sin and salvation, his clever mimicry of dialog, his witticisms and his many funny stories. A typical one was that of an old woman, arrested for the hundredth time for being drunk and disorderly, who was given the option of going to prison or being passed over to the Salvation Army. Too drunk to realize what she did, she decided for the latter. She was kindly tended to, set in a clean, cozy bed, and watched over by a sister till the morning. When she woke the sunlight streamed through the window, and the happy, unaccustomed surroundings surprised her.

"Where am I?" she asked in bewilderment.

"You are with the Salvation Army," said the sister.

"Oh, goodness gracious," roared the woman, "take me away, or I'll lose my reputation!" No wonder that most of the verbatim newspaper reports of Booth's sermons were littered with the bracketed word ("laughter!"), and no wonder, as well, that they were fascinated by the appeal and mannerisms of this "grand old man."

A COMPELLING PORTRAIT

"The general is an old man, with somewhat long and shaggy hair and beard, a hooked nose, stooped form and unprepossessing in appearance. His voice is a harsh guttural, which sounds like it was dragging over impediments as it comes to utterance. He stands with his hands behind his back, rocks his body and jerks his head. Nearly all his gestures he makes with his head. When he does use his arms, it is to throw them out in a wild, hysterical fashion. He talks in a monotone, but quite rapidly and with great energy. At times he is vehement.

"He stands in one spot most of the time, but occasionally leans far down over the desk or railing with a wild gesture when he becomes fully aroused, as in the last meeting in which he appeared; he sometimes walks from side to side, with long strides, and thrusts his long, bony arms high into the air. He is the most disagreeable speaker to whom it has been my fortune to listen, and at the same time one of the most interesting. He knows what he wants to say, and he says it with great effectiveness. He is a master of some of the arts of oratory. His theme is attractive, he is intensely in earnest, his discourse abounds in capital illustrations, and he is pretty sure to carry his audience with him." [*New York Evangelist*, April 28, 1898].

Journalists were intrigued as much by the personality as the preaching. They loved his eccentricities and puzzled somewhat that a man with only a very poor voice, and an inelegant diction, should so enthrall his listeners. One such person to attempt an analysis was the reporter for the *Milwaukee Journal*.

MASTER ORATOR

"Ten minutes after General Booth began to talk, there were probably not a dozen persons in his audience who would have said he was an orator, or even a good speaker. At that stage he was a distinct disappointment. At the close of his address of 90 minutes there were none but who were convinced that in holding the attention, arousing the interest and exciting the sympathies of an assemblage of all kinds of people, he has the skill of a master.

"General Booth has an active, nervous manner and a cheerful, hopeful way of speaking. His eyes are restless, but not shifty. At times they are quiet, one has almost said calm, and the next moment they flash in sympathy with the leader's varying word or thought. His voice is not pleasant, and this is true at all times. Often his tones are such as not to attract notice. This is when attention is concentrated on the story he is telling, or the appeal he is making, or the sin he is denouncing, or the life he is praising, but when his tone drops down again, between thoughts as it were, or when he raises his voice to reiterate a statement, or a word, which is a habit of his, its tones attract attention.

"It is not the hearty, full deep voice expected of a speaker who has addressed thousands, yet it is not the uncertain voice of the untried speaker. Last night it appeared to be the voice of a man who has used his organs of speech so much that they had begun to need tuning. Yet there was an improvement toward the end and the fear of the first few minutes that to follow him was to be an effort, was never realized.

A SPRINTER'S STANCE

"Of gesture the general had an unlimited supply. When speaking of swimming, he made with his hands those motions which every person identifies with the pursuit of that pastime; when speaking of angels, he imitated the flapping of wings; when trying to point out the volume of sin to be met with in cities, he whirled his hands about each other as if indicating an inextricable mass. Sometimes his hands were behind his back, again his arms were folded across his chest. Now his face was buried in both hands and now with one hand he stroked his long, gray beard.

"He stood sometimes on one foot, sometimes on the other, sometimes he stood in one spot, rising on his toes and heels alternately, swaying his body and shaking his head until his long locks and beard hid his face. This he varied by walking across the stage and back, and by leaning on the small railing in the front of the stage and reaching with his long arms towards the audience. Every moment introduced a new gesture. One of his oddest was when speaking of the ever-ready nature of the Army for whatever work that offered in its line, he crouched like a sprinter awaiting the starter's pistol.

"Beyond doubt General Booth is an interesting man; absorbing to those who meet him personally; delightful to those who simply hear him. As a speaker he uses a fine proportion of argument and persuasion and the combination, as he administered it last night, was convincing. He uses anecdotes and stories with great skill and fitness, most of these being simple, yet having a peculiar application to the case in point" [March 24, 1898].

Chapter Fifteen

All in all, as General Booth so readily confessed, it was highly gratifying to be so handsomely feted and so well respected. Far different was it now than it had been in 1886. In Columbus, Ohio, for example, on February 15, William Booth pauses to write: "Ten years back I visited Columbus and had a disappointing time. Then a few blood-and-fire soldiers blessed me, but the city did not know the general. On this occasion it is no exaggeration to say that it welcomed him. The main street was illuminated with electric arches and devices. The governor of the state presided at the meeting. Notwithstanding that it was ice under foot and a blizzard blowing overhead, the building, which they say seats 6,000 people, was nearly full. We had a bright time, and, I hope, a great blessing" [*War Cry*, March 12].

And in Kansas City where, a few years earlier, William Booth had been slandered, "not a ripple of dissatisfaction on account of the recent trouble, or for any reason whatever has reached me. Every man and woman has seemed to say to me, 'We are for God, our general, the Army, and the salvation of the world'" [Ibid].

On this trip, General Booth kept a daily diary for the *War Cry* and as we follow a sequence of his entries, we are treated to an intimate account of his reactions as he makes his way west. He is, as clearly seen below, delighted with everything he experiences.

What Would Paul Say?

Monday, February 2 10:40 Starting from Kansas City boarded the train for Denver, the capital of Colorado, and after a ride of 21 hours, reached the city with its 250,000 inhabitants, created within the last few years. A beautiful carriage, drawn by a pair of horses, waited at the station to drive me to the residence of Dean Hart, of the Episcopal Church, with whom I was staying. As I stepped into the carriage I could not help reminding myself of the oft-told story of the bishop who was greeted by the question on entering his equipage with its elegantly appointed liveried servants:

"Bishop, what would St. Paul in his poverty say if he saw you mounting this fine affair?"

"Well," the bishop answered, "I should think he would say that Christianity had prospered wonderfully since his day."

WASHINGTON'S BIRTHDAY

Tuesday, February 22 At 9:30 there was the usual press interview. From some cause or other these journalistic functions seem to grow more and more friendly. I usually pray with my visitors, and sometimes have a really profitable time. It was so this morning.

12:00 The Hon. Mr. Adams, governor of the state of Colorado and his lady, called to pay their respects. He appeared capable, simple, kindly and good.

3:00 The Coliseum is an enormous barn-like building, with a gallery running around. I hardly likely to guess the number it will contain, but it was full in every corner. It being the birthday of George Washington, and therefore a holiday, helped us doubtless with the crowd. Talking from one cause and another was very difficult, but God helped me to set forth, with point and power, the glorious fact that Jesus came to save His people from their sins, and 15 came out seeking to have it fulfilled in their experience.

CLEAN WORN OUT

8:00 The same place again. The governor presided, and said some very kind things about the little I have been able to do for the poor and suffering. Three-fourths of those attending were men. A prominent Catholic priest sat on the front of the platform among the leading ministers and citizens. The audience was very responsive. I talked at least an hour and 20 minutes, and had a lively time with my own soldiers in a corner of the building afterward, to which a large number of the audience, uninvited, remained including the priest before mentioned. I believe all were sorry to part with me, but I must confess to being clean worn out and glad to be able to get away, it being all I could do to get off as far as the railway depot and creep into my berth at 11:20.

Wednesday, February 23 Spent the day on the train. Was very unwell during the previous night, but gradually got round, and managed to do a little with my pen.

THREE THINGS ARE NEEDED

Thursday, February 24 Still driving along in the train, over the trackless prairies, through the valleys and over the mountains, first of Colorado, then New Mexico and then Arizona. Tonight at 6 p.m. we are to strike California—traveling miles and miles and not seeing a human habitation, and then coming on to a few humble shanties. Here and there we came on a herd of cattle looked after by the much talked-of cowboy, and here and there the hut of the red Indian, and then a group of hurriedly run-up dwellings constituting the beginnings of a future city.

It is indeed comparatively an empty country. Yet here are all but inexhaustible stores of coal and silver and copper. Here, too, are gold and precious stones, and best of all here is a soil capable of growing anything that earth can produce, together with a climate which for salubrity, invigoration and health cannot be surpassed in any part of the globe. Only three things are wanting to produce a happy and prosperous state, viz., people, water and salvation.

CITY OF ANGELS

Friday, February 25 8:30 Welcomed to Los Angeles by Lt. Colonel William Evans and a large body of officers and soldiers at the depot with shouts and blessings and music. The city has 100,000 inhabitants. Mr. Slanson, my host, tells me that when he came here 23 years ago there were only some 5,000, and 13 years back there were not more than 18,000. The chief source of prosperity of the place is its fruit, and its admirable climate for consumptives, resembling very much, I should say, the higher parts of central South Africa. On every hand you have orange groves, peach trees, vines and other kinds of fruit.

SHOUTS, TEARS, LAUGHTER

3:00 Simpson's Tabernacle, seating 2,200, was full in every part with a large number shut out for want of room. Surprised to find my old friend Mr. R.C. Morgan and his new wife, who impressed me as a kindly Christian body, waiting to shake hands with me in the ante-room. We had a real lively meeting. The soldiers shouted and wept, and laughed and listened, and prayed and sang for a couple of hours or more. Twenty-three came to the mercy seat. I am sure that I enjoyed myself, and got a blessing to my soul. I hope it was so with hundreds more.

8:00 The Coliseum, a monster building, was full from floor to the top gallery. Talking was no easy task, and my voice gave way somewhat. Still I got through, and hope, nay I am sure, a good impression was made. I was very pleased with the soldiers. Many had come long distances, and all were, I hope, refreshed, encouraged and resolved with new energy to go on with the fight.

Friday, Feb. 25, 11:00 pm. Bade good-bye to beautiful L.A., properly named so far as its situation, soft and sunny climate—for might it not become a "City of Angels"? Anyway, its people treated me very kindly, and I left them with regret.

Our train was three hours late, but a sleeping car was set aside by the kindness of the railway authorities, before its arrival in which I was thankful to deposit myself, and although the thumpings and shriekings of a railway depot at night are not very friendly to slumber, it was my happy lot to fall speedily into the arms of "tired nature's sweet restorer, balmy sleep."

Saturday, Feb. 26 was a long, sultry, dusty ride, broken only so far as I was concerned, by a 20 minute speech to a group of Salvationists and a crowd of working men at the City of Fresno on my way. How they did listen! What a satisfaction there is talking to men about salvation when they want to hear!

RED FIRES BURNING

8:15 p.m. Oakland at last! Oakland is a residential suburb of San Francisco—an arm of the sea dividing the two places. I was glad to see Oakland, and judging from the crashing of the music and the shouting of hundreds of soldiers, the burning red fires, and the smiling faces of the people, Oakland was glad to see me. Of course being two hours late spoiled the reception as arranged, and no one expected to see Mr. Mayor, but His Worship was there at the moment, and we mounted the war chariot, and I being up first introduced the mayor to the crowd, and the mayor in a few really choice and very friendly words introduced the general, who made a little speech, and then away we went to our lodging, with everybody full of joyous and blessed anticipation for the morrow.

DEATH-LIKE SILENCE

Sunday, 27th, 10:30 A large theatre was the scene of operations for the day. It was not full, a heavy downpour of rain doubtless keeping a good many strangers away, but there was a fine force of soldiers in full uniform. God helped me talk on the possibilities of faith.

Afternoon 3:00 The theatre was packed and hundreds turned away from the doors. The message was listened to with death-like silence, every sentence seemed to force its way into the hearts of the hearers.

It seemed as though the very heartthrobs of that multitude that answered back to the appeals of the Spirit of God for instantaneous and unconditional submission could be heard. The pause that followed as the voice of the speaker ceased was all but painful, and then the response came, and first one and then another decided the matter and evidenced it by coming forward. Thirty-eight yielded—one of whom, a lady, was wheeled unto the steps in a bath-chair. It was certainly one of the most effective afternoon meetings of my experience in any part of the world.

THE GOLDEN GATE

Monday, 28th Now for San Francisco! The city in which in my early days were never mentioned without calling up visions of gold-seekers and gold-finders. In company with my unflagging and intensely sympathetic helpers in this campaign, Commander and Consul Booth-Tucker, we made early for this new sphere. Surely I can say with the apostle, "Here I have no continuing city"—I am ever on the wing.

9:45 We had only a short railway ride, the train running mostly through the streets and highroads of Oakland, and then we entered one of those mammoth ferry steamers that run between these shores. I suppose the one we crossed in would contain at a push 1,000, or perhaps 1,500 people. Although not a bright day, there was sufficient sunshine to give the red soil of the two islands that stand out like giant sentinels on either side of the entrance, the imposing title of "The Golden Gate." As we steamed past I could not help looking with interest towards the harbor outside where the vast Pacific Ocean rolls her lordly waters along the shore of this continent and around the most romantically beautiful islands of the world.

A ROYAL WELCOME

In San Francisco, where William Booth was always well received, he was again treated like royalty. The *San Francisco Call* gave this lavish and very beautiful introduction to its report of his visit:

"It is the victory of the red jersey; it is the triumph of the blue bonnet. When Jan Paderewski [Polish pianist and composer] came upon the California stage the first night of his appearance here the theater was as crowded as it was yesterday when General Booth spoke. But not all the art, not all the genius of the musician could evoke the surge of enthusiasm that swept through the crowd facing the swaying figure of the tall, white-haired old Englishman who drops his h's and in his excitement forgets all about syntax, while he seizes the auditor in the grasp of his earnestness and holds his attention riveted to the religious theme he is playing upon.

CONTAGIOUS EXCITEMENT

"I never saw a more remarkable scene than that at the California theater yesterday; the great, rapt audience, murmuring and praying and groaning and sighing in a sort of ecstatic accompaniment to the speaker's appeal; the semi-obscurity of the body of the theater and the light upon the stage where General Booth sat surrounded by the officers of the Salvation Army, the speakers of the day and the band; the beautiful self-unconsciousness of the women and the grave devotion of the men; the fervor of the speakers and the responsive enthusiasm of the audience;

the pleading of the saved and the marvelous moral courage of the repentant sinner at the penitent's bench; the skillful playing on the human heart from the stage and the contagious excitement in the eager, prayerful multitude—it is an amazing, a marvelously effective picture, considered wholly apart from its religious aspect.

HANGING ON EVERY WORD

"One looks from the wonderful old man, the creator of it all, to the half-breathing house—so beloved is he, so anxious are they to hear every word—and marvels how he did it. His questions are searching. He will not pause or turn aside if words fail him. But he'll express that which has come to him though it take very fiber of his mind and of his body to do it. His words become almost living with the emphasis, the repetition, the force with which he utters them. His delivery is very inartistic, but to the power, the eloquence of it the world testifies."

FORMER "SCOUNDRELS"

The schedule of engagements in San Francisco, as elsewhere, was a taxing one: three meetings on Monday, a public lecture entitled "The Advance of the Army" on Tuesday, three on Wednesday for officers (at 10 and 3) and soldiers (at 8), and still another officers councils on Thursday before leaving for Portland. At the last of these, William Booth wrote in his diary, "There were 700 present—a few ex-soldiers amongst the rest. In front of me was one of the most interesting groups of Salvationists I ever talked to, namely, some dozen Chinese soldiers. We have in San Francisco a Chinese corps numbering 40 soldiers and 16 recruits. They were formerly amongst the biggest scoundrels in the city—murderers, thieves, opium smokers, morphine eaters, and the like. Properly saved through grace, they are kept faithful by the power of God. The corps maintains its officers and pays all working expenses. What a promise for our future operations in China!"

Sandwiched in were press interviews, private consultations, a review of recent correspondence and some time for writing, as well as a review of the troops as they marched out on several occasions. A reporter for the *Call* describes one such "procession" and by doing so gives us a fair estimation of the Army's forces in the San Francisco area.

STRENGTHENING MORALE

"The members of the different corps of the Army in the city turned out in parade last night just before the evening meeting. They assembled at the Army headquarters on Market Street, and under the folds of their flag marched down Market Street and along Kearney to Bush and to the [California] theater. There were over 500 soldiers and lassies in line, and with their bands they made an imposing show. Some of the lassies were dressed in the national costumes of many of the principal nations where the Army has its greatest strength. Many of the lassies were robed in white, and they made an attractive feature of the procession. The orphans who are protected by the organization were driven along the line of march in a bus, and they sang the familiar songs of the Army as they passed along the street."

It was, without doubt, a splendid show of strength, one which not only buoyed William Booth's spirits, but strengthened the morale of his troops and bolstered public esteem. With more than 200 new converts to his credit, several thousand dollars in donations, and no talk at all of the recent defections, William Booth left San Francisco in a happy frame of mind.

A PRISON CORPS

His only regret was that he had no time to visit the small Army corps inside San Quentin prison. Just a year earlier one had been started there by Sergeant-Major Brown of the Oakland Corps, and was now run by a "life-service" man, Adolph Braun, who also styled himself "Sergeant-Major." Though disappointed at not being visited, the Salvationists of San Quentin nevertheless sent General Booth an illuminated address:

Greeting:

To General William Booth.

Dear General,

We, the undersigned, herewith tender to you our love and good wishes.

As providence does not permit us to be personally with you in your campaign, nevertheless we shall be with you in spirit and prayer. May God abundantly bless you and prolong your life for many more years to come, are our earnest and sincere wishes.

The members of the San Quentin Salvation Army Corps.

Adolph Braun, 16,367.

Chapter Sixteen

A t eight o'clock on the evening of March 3, 1898, General Booth wrote in his diary, "We left San Francisco in a rush. John Wesley is reported to have said that he was always in haste, but never in a hurry. That is, I think, characteristic of this campaign, if not of all my doings all of the time. Not only every hour, but every minute seems to bring its accompanying duty. There is not a moment to waste.

"I think that I have seldom labored in a city with much greater satisfaction, and I am sure that I have never left with much greater reluctance. From the first welcome by the mayor of Oakland, to almost the last sympathetic word addressed to me in shaking hands with the bishop of California, friends, strangers and comrades have combined to express their respect for the Army and their good wishes for its success. My dear people said 'farewell' at the depot in a long continued storm of hallelujahs, the waving of handkerchiefs, the crashing of musical instruments, and then we were away from them, perhaps forever, as far as this life is concerned, but we are bound to come together again in the next. It must be so. But now for our 36-hour railway ride."

Friday, March 4 Still thundering along through lovely valleys. Now ascending and then descending the mountains; then passing by rude and rugged rocks, and now through some of the most beautiful and picturesque scenery of the earth.

5 p.m. Ashland is announced—a small township on the side of a mountain, with half an hour for refreshments. A few soldiers and a large crowd has assembled, consisting, I suppose, of the major portion of the adult population of this charming place. Talked to them for 20 minutes, pushing them up to seek salvation and live for heaven, the good of their fellows, and the glory of God.

I heard afterwards that the sergeant-major of the Ashland Corps, who stood before me, heard me in Missoula on my first visit to the States twelve years ago, got converted a fortnight afterwards, and there he is in full uniform, doing good service to the Army today.

7 p.m. Another wayside meeting. It was only a three-minute stop, but the conductor held the train for me to speak. The platform was packed with people, and a bank opposite. There was a great shouting and whistling, and hustling among the crowd before I made my appearance, and then all was hushed into perfect silence while I had a word with them about their souls.

Saturday, March 5 A long night, but not a very restful one; the rocking and bumping of the car was something dreadful. Had hardly got dressed in the morning before Colonel Lawley came in brandishing a telegram just received from San Francisco describing the night's meetings after we left. "All Halls Full And Twenty Souls." Hallelujah! That pleased me immensely.

9:30 a.m. Portland. Affectionate welcome from officers and soldiers and a good many strangers.

LAURELS FOR NOISE

Regarding that "affectionate welcome," *The Sunday Oregonian* (March 6) gave this fuller account:

"'Fire a volley!' commanded Major Stephen Marshall yesterday morning at the Union Depot, and a shout of greeting to the venerable leader of the Salvation Army went up that will wear the laurels for noise in staid Portland for time to come. General William Booth had not left his Pullman before the enthusiasm of his northwest soldiers was reverberating from one end of the station to the other. Two columns in close order were lined up on the west side of the track, and stretched from the powerhouse to the center of the depot building. A band organized in Portland lent discord to the greeting by joining in the hubbub.

"At 9 o'clock the Portland forces, joined to all those visiting from the cities of the entire Northwest, mustered at Columbia Hall, on First Street, and marched to the depot. In double file the column reached a distance of over three blocks. The colors of the different corps enlivened the line and gave the marchers a warlike aspect as their steady tread was heard from the asphalt pavement. When the depot was reached, the column filed through to the platform, the privilege being granted by the terminal company in order that the general might see his troops in martial array when first looking from his car. The platform has contained no more people at one time, nor has there ever been a higher spirit of gladness and joy from its burden than rose from the wearers of the red jerseys and poke bonnets.

SHOWING NO RESTRAINT

"But a few moments after schedule time—9:30—the Southern rolled into the depot and the excitement of the waiting soldiers became intense. As each coach passed their position, the windows were eagerly scanned by countless eyes in search of a Salvation Army emblem. When the Pullman bearing the general and his traveling companions came to a halt, and the familiar figure of Commander Booth-Tucker swung from the platform, there was a wild shout. As each of the other members of the party, save the general, came forth, the bottled enthusiasm seemed about to break the dam and deluge the depot.

"When finally the gaunt frame of a man nearing 70 years of age, over six feet in height, wearing a high beaver, a red jersey and military coat, and conspicuous by a flowing, patriarchal beard, stepped nimbly from the platform, there was no restraint. Had there been any doubt from this figure's appearance, there could have been none from his action. The depot platform had but been reached when the general raised his hat in the air and gave a hallelujah shout that was unmistakable. The response was deafening, and several moments elapsed before the air was sufficiently composed to give the ears a respite."

FREE AND FULL SALVATION

An hour after he arrived, and having been seen to his lodging (the home of the Rev. Dr. Edgar P. Hill), William Booth was hard at work conducting officers councils ("70 officers of as good, loyal and devoted a spirit as are to be found within four corners of the Army"). On Sunday (March 6), at the Baptist Church, at least 3,000 people listened to his sermon on "free and full salvation." It was a fine, big building, but only by lifting up the side with a winch arrangement could it accommodate the large crowd.

"It was difficult for talking," General Booth admitted, "but God helped me, hundreds were convicted, and 19 came out to the penitent-form, seeking salvation. I hear that after I had finished, the pastor met in an adjoining room with a number of young people who had been impressed during the service, and 20 stood up signifying their desire to lead a Christian life." At 3 and 6 p.m. the Marquam Grand Opera House was "crowded to the ceiling" by Portlanders eager, in the afternoon, to listen to his lecture of the "advance of the Army" and, in the evening, to experience a genuine Salvation Army worship service. In that they were not disappointed.

GOLD FEVER

In many respects, then, the public receptions, the lectures and the meetings of the 1898 tour were very similar to those of 1894, already described in the preceding chapter. What was noticeably different was the mood of the country itself. In the West, through which William Booth traveled during the last week of February and the first week of March, all the talk was of gold—gold to be had for the taking in the Klondike. While in the East, as we shall soon see, the main topic on everyone's lips—in the newspapers and even in the pulpits—was "war with Spain."

As for the first concern ("craze" might be a better word), William Booth met it head on when his entourage entered Seattle on the night of March 7. He soon found that as many as 10,000 men were in the city, buying outfits, booking passage, and preparing for the hazardous journey to Alaska. Many just like them—as many as 40,000 from all over the world—had been doing so since about July 1897 when news of the Klondike "gold strikes" reached the United States, and the famous "Klondike Stampede" had started. Fewer than half of them ever saw any gold, and many of them (of those who didn't turn back) died of exposure, exhaustion and starvation. It was a "mad, mad" rush of feverish men, most too foolish to realize their own folly. At the moment of William Booth's visit, a large number were in Seattle, awaiting their transportation north.

KLONDIKE OR BUST

For a brief while they left off their Klondike busyness and crowded to the train depot to greet the man whose reputation for good deeds had preceded him. "An amusing incident occurred as the general stepped down from the car. The usual outburst of enthusiasm greeted the general from his people and friends, and, as he walked down the platform with the Consul and the Field Commissioner (Eva Booth, who had crossed from Victoria to escort her father back to Canada), a big brawny, bronzed miner shouted "Klondyke or Bust, General."

When William Booth mounted the temporary platform to speak to the men—"men on the sidewalks, men peering from the balconies and window sills, men impeding the traffic, crowding Klondyke outfit stores, all intent upon the movements of the general"—he looked over the vast crowd, and said to the mayor who had come to welcome him, "*This is my Klondyke!*"

"It was," wrote the *War Cry* correspondent, "an interesting spectacle—those figures on the rough platform, the red lights of the corps' torches flashing across the dark field of humanity, the mayor breaking into a poetic effusion as he welcomed the general—stately, picturesque, and calm." And, as the crowd fell silent, William Booth thundered: "I am on my way to the Klondyke. My Klondyke is the Kingdom of God. What is yours?" The meeting which followed was a huge success.

On the streets of Seattle and on the jetty from which he took his departure for Vancouver, General Booth witnessed the thousands of men smitten with gold fever. And here he immediately agreed to the proposals submitted to him by his daughter, Eva, to equip a Salvation Army Klondike expedition. "It was beautiful to meet my dear Eva again," he wrote in his diary, "and to find her keeping so much better in health. Like the rest of the world in these parts, I found her full of the Klondyke! She is planning for an expedition to save the souls of the miners while they are seeking the gold. God bless her!"

EVA'S EMPATHY

Eva, of course, had come well prepared. In a brief, which her father read as he traveled to Victoria, British Columbia, she wrote:

"As I have watched crowds of those men, many so young and some old, with songs of pleasure on their lips, descend the gangway of the emigrant steamer, and shout their good-byes to companions, and as I have also seen them in the over-crowded cars and depots, during my present Northwestern campaign, my heart has ached with desire to be with them on the field, 'midst the dangers that threaten and the sorrows that await them, to help stem the tides of disappointments and temptations dark and terrible, which are bound to come thick and fast to thousands, and save them by the conquering grace and dying love of Jesus.

"For what, alas! is before them to relieve the wretched monotony of their lives? Nothing but whiskey and the gamblers' table, with all the horrors that follow in the train of these body-wasting and soul-destroying agencies. Although gold abounds, want is dire and painful, for food is scarce, disease is at work, and sin is rampant, hurrying on, as always, with its consequences cruel and bitter."

IMPLEMENTING EVA'S PLAN

So impressed was William Booth by his daughter's proposal, with its detailed statements of expenses and supplies, and so touched was he by the sight of the prospective gold-seekers in Seattle, that he immediately agreed. And, within a month, a Salvation Yukon field force, consisting of six male officers and two female nurses, had set out from Toronto, eventually to labor up the steep Chilkoot Pass and then down the Yukon River to Dawson City which they reached on June 25. To the nearly 30,000 people crowded into its small confines, the Salvationists were indeed a godsend. Only about half of them, writes one historian, bothered to look for gold. Of those who did only about 4,000 found any. Of these only a few hundred found enough to make them rich.

Thus the streets of Dawson City were filled with thousands of aimless men, many without the courage to return home empty-handed, more with no money to do so even if they wished, imprisoned in a town of false-fronted saloons where whisky was cheaper than wholesome food. Among these the Salvation Army "Klondikers" set to work, not only building a small meeting hall and residence but a shelter as well. Soon long lines of stranded and sick gold-seekers filled the shelter to its capacity, and the services of the Army nurses, especially during the outbreaks of typhoid and scurvy, were greatly appreciated. It was not, strictly speaking, an American enterprise, but its impetus was secured on the streets of Seattle during William Booth's visit and many of the recipients of the Army's caring were American gold-seekers.

Chapter Seventeen

From the balmy regions of Los Angeles to the slushy confines of Seattle, William Booth turned eastward again to face the bitter cold of the American prairies. Strangely enough, the old man was not at all unhappy with that prospect. In fact he seemed to prefer the cold weather to the warm. He did not, he often said, like the heat of summer, and though he appreciated the warmth of Los Angeles, he was not at all unhappy with the cooler (some might say infinitely colder) regions of the north. It might be noted that his first visit in 1886 was in October through December. In 1894-95 he chose October to February, a time-frame which, on the prairies at least, would have required a pair of wooly "long-johns." And in 1898 his January to March schedule certainly had his soldiers sloshing through the snow on their welcome marches and saw him "reluctantly relaxing" as his train plowed through the snowdrifts.

UNEXPECTED INTERLUDE

On the trip from Spokane to Winnipeg (March 14-16), the general's party encountered one of the worst blizzards of the year, 300 miles west of Grand Forks, North Dakota. The snowdrifts were five-feet high. "Fortunately no accidents otherwise marred the journey, excepting that one of the party, pooh-poohing the warning of a brakeman, went to examine the snow-plough, and got buried for two minutes in a snowdrift. These snowdrifts resemble sin—very alluring, inviting and apparently free of danger, until you walk into them, and then—down you go. The secretary will remember that snowdrift." After a 10-hour delay, during which the snowplows finally forced their way through a mountain of snow, they got as far as Grand Forks but too late to catch the Minneapolis mail train going north to Winnipeg. But Winnipeg's disappointment was Grand Forks' blessing.

"At 10 a.m.," wrote the *War Cry* correspondent, "we got a wire on the cars, signed by Dr. J.R. Church, to the following effect—*General Booth—You cannot get to Winnipeg tonight. May I arrange a meeting here?*' At 11:30 we replied:

"*Dr. Church—Have not yet abandoned hope of catching connection for Winnipeg. If possible, however, will gladly do a meeting. Rush all necessary arrangements!—GENERAL.*

"We hadn't the slightest idea, when we dispatched that message, who Dr. Church was. We only knew that there were neither P.O., D.O., nor F.O. [various officers] on the ground. They were all in Winnipeg."

HAVE NO FEAR

The train reached Grand Forks at four p.m. In the unexpected crowd which waited in fur coats was one man who attracted notice: powerfully built, looking more fifty than sixty, with a bronzed face. He looked somewhat austere—until he smiled and then his face radiated energy and action. This was Dr. Church, local veterinary surgeon and treasurer of the Army corps. And he could speak.

"Listen to him," writes the astounded *War Cry* reporter: 'Welcome to Grand Forks, General. Delighted and sorry for Winnipeg, but the Lord is in it. It's all right. Here, John. Take the general to the rig. Bill, throw these valises into the rig. Harry, take the secretaries to the quarters—the general and the commissioner go to my house. That's right! I guess we are about straight for tonight. I've got the biggest church in the place for the meeting. You will have to speak on the Army, General. Rev. Gifford will be chairman. Do the people know? Everyone knows. I got it into the evening papers. The boys have been around the city with dodgers. I got it announced in all the schools—children are the cheapest and best advertisers in the world. Don't fear. We have no charges. We will pack the building.'"

Even William Booth, the supreme go-getter, was impressed by Dr. Church. But who was he, he wanted to know? The general was soon provided with an answer. Dr. Church, whose father was a veterinarian and who brought up his son to the same profession, was born among the Thousand Islands. He succeeded in his profession, amassed a fortune, but drank it all—"for ten years he consumed a dollar in whiskey and a dollar in cigars daily, fought and gambled." Three years ago he had entered the Army barracks in Grand Forks, was convicted, converted, and had been a Salvationist ever since.

A BOUNTIFUL SPREAD

It was, all agreed, one of the most pleasant surprises of the trip. The supper provided by Dr. Church, though not much to William Booth's frugal tastes, was most welcome to the other members of the party. "The doctor overdid it," wrote Alex Nichol, "but the overflowing generosity of his heart led him astray. We forgive him. The spread was bewildering. The secretaries, who are in danger of treating chicken, in all shapes and sizes, as a necessity of existence, were amazed. For supper I observed: oyster soup, cold meat, cold ham, vegetables ad lib, oranges, apples, bananas, tea, coffee, cream, etc.

A MELTING POT

"The Grand Forks Corps," he continued, "is in a creditable condition, and affords a fine illustration of the successful working of one of the principles which has given the United States such a unique and commanding position in the world. I call it the doctrine of 'assimilation.' If the body assimilates food well, it becomes healthy and vigorous. In North Dakota you have the assimilation under one flag, of a variety of races—Swedes, Norwegians, Germans, and Russians—with the result that you have growing up here evidently a fine race. I was told that the son of a Bohemian took our luggage to the buggy; a Norwegian drove the general to his lodging; a Swede took charge of the secretaries; an Englishman led one of the party to the hairdresser; and a Scotchman— the illustration would not be perfect without—looked after the money.

"And just as, under the American constitution, representatives of all nationalities are welcome to share its privileges, laws, and protection, so under our Salvation Army umbrella all peoples are learning to love each other, and live for each other in the spirit of the Son of Man. Grand Forks is an international corps, has the international spirit, and is yet true to itself, and true to the state and country under which it fights."

In the evening, snowbound though Grand Forks was, the church was crowded to the door. "The general was A-1. He had a great time.

People were delighted with his happy, humorous, trenchant style. One man describing to another at the depot next morning, said, 'Oh, he is quite different to what I expected. The general compels you to stop. I could have listened to him till now.'" Though the Field Commissioner from Canada, William Booth's daughter Eva, was "in an agony" the whole time because of her disappointed officers in Winnipeg, the rest of the party had a wonderful time—Grand Forks was a perfect consolation, and the interlude was one of those happenstances which made the tour much more memorable.

FRIENDS FROM CORNWALL

In fact, William Booth seemed to enjoy his small-town visits. After he had returned from his side trip to Winnipeg, and had bombarded Minneapolis, St. Paul and Milwaukee (where he was rewarded with "one of the most triumphant meetings of his campaign"), the general made another side-trip to the twin mining towns of Ishpeming and Red Jacket, Michigan—the former made wealthy by iron and the latter by copper.

The main reason, we learn, is that in both places there were quite a few miners who had emigrated from Cornwall and who (or whose parents) had known General Booth in his early preaching days. "Here are located," he wrote, "a large number of my old friends, the Cornishmen, many of whom cherished, I am informed, very kindly recollections of the labors of my dear wife and self in that country 35 and 36 years ago. It was a long way to go to see them, involving as it did a three days' journey, but the disappointment was so great on account of my not visiting them three years ago that the commander said he really dare not see their faces again if they did not take me this time."

SHORING UP CHICAGO

From there it was back to Chicago where the Army—now with the largest following in the country—had suffered its greatest losses as a result of the Ballington Booth defection two years earlier. It was here, in his officers and soldiers meetings, that William Booth looked forward to boosting the morale of those who had remained faithful and encouraging backsliders to return to the fold.

"To meet my Chicago braves once more," General Booth wrote, "and congratulate them on having been brought in faithfulness and security through the stormy troubles of the last two years, was an anticipation that I dwelt upon with no little satisfaction from the first moment the campaign was resolved upon. The meeting proved that the feeling was mutual. The welcome was a bit of real heart enthusiasm. At least 800 soldiers were awaiting me, and the greeting they gave me can never be forgotten. Wave after wave of holy gladness seemed to roll over the crowd.

RED HOT WELCOME

"Musical instruments were blown, drums were beaten, hands clapped, but loud above all were the reiterated volleys of 'Amen!' 'God bless you!' and 'Hallelujah!' and then when, after repeated attempts at order on the part of Colonel Lawley, who was on the bridge, the delighted crowds dismounted the forms, resumed their seats and quieted their excited spirits, a brother or a sister would call out 'God bless the general!' and the fury of the red-hot welcome that was burning in every heart burst out again.

"At last, however, we got to business, and had one of the most enjoyable bits of talk I have done for many a day, and I am glad to say, not only enjoyable, but useful, for after we had got back to the stern realities of a soldier's life and a soldier's work, and pointed out the Laodiceanism and shortcomings and backslidings with which some unfortunately mar and disfigure it, and the hanging back of others, [shunning] holy power and desperate fighting which is their privilege. We demanded instant surrender. Forty-four knelt at the mercy seat. A number of ex-soldiers were amongst the number. It will be a joy in the memory of many forever, and the story will be talked over generations yet to come" [*War Cry*, April 23, 1898].

Chapter Eighteen

With Chicago secure once again, William Booth turned his attention to the eastern United States—to Boston, Philadelphia, Buffalo and New York. But, by the time he did so (between April 10 and 27, 1898), the nation was on a war alert. The newspapers hardly found space to report General Booth's activities, so demanding were the reports of war in Cuba—of the need to support the Cubans in their fight for independence against Spain.

The nationalist revolt against Spanish imperialism in Cuba had begun a few years earlier, around April 1895. The United States had been sympathetic to the rebel cause but had been reluctant to get involved. On January 25, 1898, however, ostensibly to protect its interests in Cuba, the American government sent a warship, the U.S. Maine, to Havana. When, on February 15, the Maine was destroyed by an explosion which killed 266 sailors, the yellow newspapers, blaming it on the Spanish (though that was doubtful), called for military intervention.

On April 11, therefore, after much public pressure, President McKinley asked Congress for the authority to send in American troops and, as a response, Spain declared war on the United States on April 23 in the midst of William Booth's six-day campaign in New York.

Ultimately, the Cuban war was of short duration (April to August 1898), and America was easily victorious. While it did gain Cuba its independence, some 3,300 Americans died during the conflict (nearly 3,000 of them from tropical diseases). At the same time the United States, intoxicated by the idea of expansionism, fought to free other Spanish territories (the Philippines, Guam and Puerto Rico), some of which were taken over as American protectorates. It was, as many historians have pointed out, the beginning of American imperialism and of its role as a world power.

POLITICAL ASTUTENESS

It was quite natural, then, that William Booth should be asked his opinions concerning the impending war with Spain. And, again, he demonstrated great political acumen in his comments to reporters on the issue. He was, in fact, very knowledgeable about the political situation in the United States, and quite prescient in his views about the country's future. As for war itself, he believed it was inherently evil but recognized that, faced with unwarranted aggression, people and nations, at times, had no choice but to defend themselves.

As for the impending war itself, General Booth pleaded for peace and a possible arbitration of the Spanish-American impasse. "All good men must deplore the terrible condition of affairs in Cuba. But to widen the area of suffering by another war would, it seems to me, aggravate the evil a thousand times over, seeing that it would only involve a much larger multitude in greater suffering. But whatever pacific influences can be brought by the nations of Christendom would surely be both desirable and praiseworthy. By all means let America take the lead. That God will guide those who are in authority is the Army's prayer" [*New York World*, Feb. 14, 1898].

More specifically, William Booth felt that Spain was wrong in not allowing Cuban independence and believed that if the United States took a strong stand Spain would back down. And when war seemed inevitable (as it did just before he left America), he saw the Army's role as a reliever of suffering and promised to send nurses to the American military camps and to Cuba itself if allowed. A message, offering such support, was sent to President McKinley.

The offer was accepted and, almost immediately, officer-padres and officer-nurses were making their way to military camps in Florida and Georgia to provide civilian assistance to lonely troops. The Army's active and ready involvement was not only a sign of its acceptance in the American community but a precursor of the role it would assume in two world wars. The presence of William Booth in America at that moment was a major factor in such action.

Perhaps his most significant insight, certainly indicative of William Booth's clear-sighted view of world affairs, came when he was asked whether he thought the world was getting better. He shook his head and said, "Europe is today an armed camp, and America is fast getting that way." This country, he thought, would never again be on a peace footing, but would continue its war preparations in such a manner as to show to the world hereafter that it must not be attacked with impunity. "You are a mighty nation,'" he said, "an object lesson for the world. You are the young eagle whose strength no man can measure, for as yet you have never been tried. When you get your army and your navy the nations of the world will stand aghast" [*The North American*, April 13, 1898]. It was, given America's ultimate rise to power, a very astute assessment of its future.

MARCH OF WITNESS

Though the Cuban war was a constant distraction, and certainly drove William Booth to the back pages of New York newspapers, his final days in that city were ones of considerable exertion—a week-long "Great Salvation Campaign." Salvationists from 50 miles around had gathered to savor the religious experience. On the Tuesday evening of his arrival (April 19) the general delivered an address on the work of the Army in Carnegie Hall at which there was a "chorus of one thousand voices, floods of music" and enough special guests (Hon. Theodore Roosevelt, Hon. Seth Low, Dr. Josiah Strong and many others) to make any Salvationist proud. This was followed by four days of officers and soldiers councils, culminating in a giant "march-of-witness."

"There were," stated the *New York World*, "about 1,500 people in the parade and all in Salvation uniform. There were three bands and several floats. The procession started at Broadway and Forty Seventh Street and ended at Union Square, where an open-air meeting was held . . . Four flag-bearers, two with United States and two with Salvation Army flags, headed the procession. Following them were members of the staff on horseback. 'Joe the Turk' in a suit of bright red, and his famous umbrella headed the first band. Everybody cheered the general as the line passed on. Ever so many bandsmen performed the difficult feat of waving their caps without missing a note. General Booth smiled benignly and acknowledged each salute with a curious waving of his right hand.

"The first float illustrated the work of the salvage brigade. Then came a float labeled 'Knights of Hope' with two men in convict garb and Salvation lassies offering them sympathy and *War Crys*. The Rescue brigade had a float and it was a very realistic picture of one of the miserable places where the slum brigade works. There was a float of children in sailor garb, one representing the hospital work.

"Perhaps about a thousand people crowded around the stand in Union Square. When General Booth appeared they saluted him with a volley, which, of course, is a cheer. The drums rolled and the bands tooted to add to the noise. General Booth spoke for about five minutes and then retired.

"There was much singing, five minute speeches by different officers being interspersed. No reference was made to the war [in Cuba] save in

Commander Booth's closing prayer, when he referred to it very briefly. The band struck up 'The Star Spangled Banner,' and a young woman sprang to the platform and waved an American flag, but there was not much enthusiasm over it" [April 24].

CAMPAIGN FINALE

On Sunday and Monday (April 24 and 25), General Booth preached at three "salvation" meetings each day in the Army's own Memorial Hall and in the Academy of Music. And on Tuesday he presided over a "Mammoth Social Demonstration" in the Metropolitan Opera House which again was supported by many leading citizens and chaired by the ex-Secretary of the Navy, Benjamin F. Tracy. So, with a fitting conclusion to nearly four months of strenuous campaigning, and a sense of great accomplishment, on the following day General Booth set sail once again for England.

The 1898 tour had, William Booth declared, been an astounding success. As far as the Army was concerned, he felt he had healed many wounds (especially those of a disaffected public), had regained the confidence of many of America's influential supporters, had endeared himself again to the American press, and had helped boost the morale of his soldiers to a level higher than ever before. He sanctioned a "Klondike expedition" which his daughter, Eva, would see successfully put into action. He had taken a personal interest in the creation of at least two farm colonies and had signed their deeds of purchase.

He had supported America's Cuban-war effort by sending officer padres and nurses to various military camps and, finally, he had, to a large extent, counteracted the negative publicity occasioned by the defection of his son, Ballington. Indeed, by the time he left America, in fact, it had all but disappeared from the minds of most journalists. And, though the friction between the two organizations was still evident in some towns ("why do they have to hold open-airs opposite each other at the same time," lamented one observer), it would soon become apparent that the Volunteers would soon be overshadowed by the Salvation Army.

On a very personal level, William Booth had thoroughly enjoyed having his two daughters, Emma and Eva, at his side for so many weeks. Eva was, by temperament, much like her father while Emma, he made it known, was very much like her mother. Though both were precious to him, Emma seemed his favorite, so placid, so calm, so efficient. While Bramwell was, he often said, his "right hand," Emma was his left. While on this tour, their affection for each other was always obvious as she, at almost every meeting, gently assisted him by taking his arm and leading him to the platform, where she stayed almost always by his side. As a number of reporters stated, to see father and daughter together, so closely aligned in the work of rescuing the lost, so supportive of each other in revival meetings, was a great inspiration to most American families.

Visit 4: 1902-03

The Restless Heart

My Lord, what am I and what is my Father's house that Thou shouldst have raised up round the world such a host of brave, self-sacrificing, capable men and women to assist me to carry out my wishes, to obey my commands, to run at my bidding, and be willing to suffer and die for the sake of the flag—the flag that I have hoisted over their hearts? Who am I that I should have the privilege of commanding such a brave, heroic, and mighty host?

—William Booth's farewell speech before
leaving for America (1902)

1902-03 Itinerary

Arrived NY Oct. 4, 1902

New York Oct. 4-10

Canada Oct. 11-Nov. 5

Buffalo, NY Nov. 8-9

Conneaut, Ohio Nov. 10

Columbus, Ohio Nov. 11

Detroit, Mich. Nov. 12

Toledo, Ohio Nov. 13

Chicago, Ill. Nov. 15-21

St. Paul / Minneapolis Nov. 22-24

Milwaukee, Wis. Nov. 25

Duluth, Minn. Nov. 27

Grand Forks, ND Nov. 28

Winnipeg Nov. 29-Dec. 3

Des Moines, Iowa Dec. 5-7

Kansas City, Mo. Dec. 8-11

Denver, Co. Dec. 14-15

Colorado Springs, Co. Dec. 16

Los Angeles, Ca. Dec. 18-19

Santa Barbara [resting]
Dec. 20-26

San Francisco, Ca. Dec. 27

Oakland, Ca. Dec. 28

San Francisco Dec. 29-Jan 1

Salt Lake City, Utah Jan. 4-5

Omaha, Neb. Jan. 7

St. Joseph, Mo. Jan. 8

St. Louis, Mo. Jan. 10-14

Cincinnati, Ohio Jan. 15-16

Cleveland, Ohio Jan. 17-22

Pittsburgh, Penn. Jan. 25

Chattanooga, Tenn. Jan 27

Nashville, Tenn. Jan. 28

Memphis, Tenn. Jan. 29

Dallas, Texas Feb. 1

New Orleans, La. Feb. 3

Mobile, Al. Feb. 4-5

Birmingham, Al Feb. 7

Atlanta, Ga. Feb. 9-10

Washington, DC Feb. 11-13

Philadelphia, Penn. Feb. 14-16

Worcester, Mass. Feb. 20

Boston, Mass. Feb. 21-23

Resting & business Feb. 24-28

New York City March 1-7

Chapter Nineteen

On April 10, 1902, William Booth celebrated his seventy-second birthday. He should, perhaps, have been content at that age to rest from his life's labors—satisfied that he had brought into existence one of the world's great religious/social agencies; that it was now being capably cared for by his eldest son, Bramwell. Perhaps he should have been enjoying the pleasures of his London garden or having tea (which he loved so much) and long chats with old friends.

William Booth had a restless heart—consumed, as he put it, with such a passion for souls that could not, would not, rest until the whole world was brought to the Army's mercy seat. "I am tired," he wrote, "but must go on—on—on. I cannot stand still. A 'fire' is in my bones!"

And so, in October 1902, after returning from an inspection of his troops in France, Germany, Holland, Denmark, Norway, Switzerland and Italy, he again sailed across the Atlantic, bound for one of his favorite destinations—North America.

But it was not passion alone that drove him. According to his biographer, Harold Begbie, he had a compulsion to keep working, keep moving among his troops, partly to conquer his fear of old-age loneliness and partly to relieve the pain and bewilderment that was now beginning to fill his heart. Not so much from any physical deterioration, for he was still relatively robust, as from bouts of melancholia and heart sickness. Death had recently claimed some of his closest acquaintances, friends and relatives: Cecil Rhodes, James Dowdle (who had been with him on his first trip to America), and his sister, Mary, had all just died. But, much more soul searing were the defections of his children.

CATHERINE AND HERBERT

Ballington and Maud had started the trend in 1896 when they had refused his "farewell orders" and, after much public wrangling, had left to start their own Army-styled organization, The Volunteers of America. In January and May of 1902, his brilliant daughter, Catherine, and his talented son, Herbert, also tendered their resignations. Catherine had little choice: her husband, Arthur Booth-Clibborn, for some years in disagreement with William over the issue of pacifism, had recently thrown in his lot with the infamous faith healer, Dr. John Dowie. For Catherine it was either leave the Army or leave her husband.

Herbert's resignation was more straightforward. He had simply grown tired of being controlled from distant London. His disillusionment came to a crisis during his command of Australia, and from there he and his wife, Cornelie, moved around the world as itinerant evangelists.

CHOSEN BY GOD

William Booth said, "My precious children have helped me [make the Army] . . . I say they have helped me; but the Army does not belong to the Booth family. It belongs to the Salvation Army. So long as the Booth family are good Salvationists, and worthy of commands, they shall have them, but only if they are. I am not the general of the family. I am the general of the Salvation Army."

DESTINY

It may have been, then, that William Booth's urge to travel was a defiant rejection of old age and an antidote to pain and loneliness, but we must understand that it also stemmed from a genuine belief that it was his destiny, through the Salvation Army, to convert the whole world. He believed, as Harold Begbie asserts, "that it was possible to bring men and women of every degree and temperament into the fold of the Salvation Army, and he even dared, in certain moments of enthusiasm, to think that he himself might live to accomplish this consummation . . . The older he grew and the more deep became his knowledge of mankind, the more did this sorrowful man yearn to convert humanity from the folly of a transitory world to the eternal satisfaction of the world to come. And at this time the idea flamed in his soul of converting not hundreds here and thousands there, but all the world" [*Begbie*, II: 251-52].

A UNIVERSAL INSTITUTION

The positive receptions accorded him on his previous visits to Australia, India, and North America, Begbie argues, helped to entrench that belief. Thus, in 1902 William Booth was a man driven as much as ever, perhaps more than ever, by an intense passion to make the Army a truly universal institution—one which would transcend all boundaries of race, color and politics.

And the one nation, above all others, where "universal salvation" would see its greatest success would be the United States. Some might call it sheer egotism, but, if one reads his statements carefully, one can see that General Booth (though perhaps overestimating his appeal) was totally sincere in his belief. Perhaps the ready support of the American people—even of their presidents and politicians—their eager embrace of his evangelical style, or even the wide open spaces awaiting an Army flag, may have influenced his thinking. But, whatever it was, William Booth believed that the United States would be the country, especially in the burgeoning West and South, where the Salvation Army would become the leading religious denomination.

A MIGHTY CAMPAIGN

"Taking into consideration," he told reporters, "the reception on my arrival, the friendliness of the press, and the general evidences of enthusiastic loyalty on the part of my people, I believe that there is every promise for a mighty campaign throughout the entire country, and for raising as strong an Army in the United States as can be found in any country under our flag. I am more in love with America than ever" [*NY Times*, Oct. 6]. Such were the dreams of this elderly, now lionized, religious leader as he again set foot on American soil.

In 1902, the Salvation Army in America was 23 years old and was well on its way to becoming, whether William Booth liked it or not, a thoroughly American institution. And, as such, it was ready to greet him in typically American fashion—with extravagant fanfare and plenty of hoopla.

FIREWORKS, FLAGS, AND BANDS

Indeed, royalty could not have been greeted with greater fervor—or with greater spectacle—than was William Booth when he arrived in New York on October 4 aboard the American steamship *Philadelphia*. Twelve tugboats and three side-wheel passenger boats, packed with almost 2,000 Salvationists, had set out at 6:30 a.m. and an hour later had pulled up next to the *Philadelphia* as she lay anchored at the quarantine station awaiting customs clearance. When the general, his breakfast unfinished, rushed to the starboard rail, the tugboats began to toot their whistles and the Salvationists sang to the accompaniment of several brass bands; they shouted and set off firecrackers, and generally raised their welcome to the skies.

Here is how Colonel Alex Nichol, the *War Cry* correspondent, described the scene: "We arrived at Sandy Hook soon after midnight on Friday, anchoring at the quarantine station at about 2 a.m. By seven o'-clock, before the ship's bill of health had been passed, the sound of bombs [firecrackers] was heard. The passengers rushed on deck eager to know what was happening, and noticed in the distance a fleet of steamers, decorated with flags of welcome from end to end, and loaded with shouting, cheering, enthusiastic Salvationists, who, after being up a good part of the night, had made an early start to give their general a loyal, hearty welcome to their country, and accompany his steamer in royal fashion from the quarantine station to the American company's landing-stage.

DEFYING DESCRIPTION

"The sights and sounds connected with this reception are altogether beyond my power to describe. Every conceivable device in the direction of sound-producing instruments, and that hearty enthusiasm peculiar to Salvationists [and particularly to *American* Salvationists, he might have said], were brought into full play. Imagine the sirens or hooters of a dozen steamers (not all in the same key) going full blast all at one time.

Add to this the explosion of bombs, rockets, and daylight fireworks. Add again the music of Salvation Army bands, and the shouts of welcome of officers and soldiers from the various departments of the national headquarters, the social work, the central, western, New York, New England, and Ohio and German provinces—and a distant imagination of what took place is just possible.

So Many Good People

"I have been present at many notable events in Army history, but I have never seen anything after this kind before. It is not too much to say that it was unique. One of our rich passengers, a New York banker, remarked to me that he had never seen 'so many good people together before.' Another said it reminded him of the reception accorded to Admiral Dewey upon his return from the Spanish War. A third remarked that, in his judgment, 'it beat the Coronation hollow.' There was not an unkind word, notwithstanding the fact that some of the passengers had to walk about with their hands to their ears owing to the great noise, although they were smiling with pleasure all the time" [*Begbie*, II: 241-42].

And here is how General Booth, in whose honor the whole startling affair had been staged, felt about his welcome as he reported it in a letter to his son Bramwell:

"Sometime in the middle of the night we came to anchor in what is termed the quarantine ground. Here we waited till daylight for the inspection of the officer of health. No vessel being allowed to go further up the bay, much less to come alongside the wharf of the city, without this gentleman's certificate as to there being no contagious disease on board . . .

"We were up and about pretty early. Breakfast was announced for six, but was not ready till 7:30. Everybody was more or less excited at the prospect of being so much nearer Home Sweet Home, as the bulk of the 1st and 2nd saloon and many of the steerage passengers were returning from pleasure or family trips to Europe.

"While dealing with the good things before us suddenly a burst of shouting and singing and other sounds of enthusiasm came through the saloon windows and fetched everybody to their feet. What could it be? . . . The question was soon answered—it is the Salvation Army come to greet their general.

EUPHORIA

"I have had welcomes almost innumerable and of the most varied character in many parts of the world, but never anything which for enthusiasm and gladness surpassed that given me by the excited Salvationists that crowded the 11 steamers who came down the New York water on that Saturday morning. I cannot find time to describe. I cannot tell how many press men I spoke to, or how many times I was photographed, or how many greetings I received and returned, or how my heart leapt within me when dear Fritz [Commissioner Booth-Tucker] came on board in the revenue cutter, or when my dear precious Emma stepped on the steamer as we came alongside the wharf.

"By 10:00 I had reached headquarters, and in a few minutes was meeting a group of reporters. Before I was through with them, the banging of drums and the explosion of the bombs, which with deafening bangs followed one another in repeated succession, proclaimed the approach of the procession of the officers and soldiers who had followed through the city from the steamers on which they had been down the bay.

DAY OF DAYS

"It was really an impressive march—headed and accompanied by the police, as drum after drum and department after department filed under the balcony on which I stood. My whole soul was drawn out in response to the loving looks and greetings they sent up to me there.

"That through, I finished my interview with the press, which the arrival of the procession had interrupted, and after dealing with their catechizing, I sat down to luncheon with several leading press gentlemen of higher importance . . . It was a day of days, one of the most remarkable of my life."

And so would be the days ahead. The outpouring of public adulation surpassed anything that William Booth had hitherto received, and sometimes bordered on idolatry. Here, for example, is a rather effusive but not atypical example of American editorials from the *Des Moines Daily News* (Dec. 6):

"'One of the arrivals on the steamship Philadelphia,' says a New York newspaper, 'is General William Booth of the Salvation Army.' One of the arrivals! This vessel never before carried so great a man as this tall, gaunt, white-haired, white-bearded organizer, enthusiast, and men-lover. Wherever the sun rises there is heard the morning song of the Salvation Army. Wherever the sun sets is heard its drumbeat. Wherever men and women suffer and sorrow and despair; wherever little children moan and hunger, there are the disciples of William Booth.

REMINISCENT OF LINCOLN

"The man's heart is big enough to take in the world. He has made the strongest distinct impact upon human hearts of any man living. This is a man of the Lincoln type. Like Lincoln he has the saving grace of humor and sense of proportion . . .

Archimedes said, 'Give me lever and a fulcrum and I will move the world.' Human hearts make the fulcrum of William Booth and love is the lever. With these he is slowly lifting a large part of this weary, heartsick, hopeless and despairing world. Blessings on this good, grey head which all men know!"

It was lavish praise indeed. And, though many Americans had seen and heard William Booth before, and in spite of the fact that his sermons were still the same, and his public lectures on the same topic, "The Past, Present, and Future of the Salvation Army"—in spite of the familiarity (which, in his case, never did breed contempt), more people than ever thronged to his meetings.

CARNEGIE HALL MOB SCENE

At the three salvation meetings at the Academy of Music on Sunday, October 5, more than 8,000 people "listened to his pleadings" and at the Monday public lecture 4,000 filled the Carnegie Music Hall. "The police had prepared for a crowd," wrote a reporter, "but the size of it exceeded their expectations. Several times they closed the doors to check the crush. In spite of the precaution several women fainted. They were resuscitated, but they insisted on going in. The general scramble had for a short time a very threatening appearance. At least 1,000 persons were turned away" [NY Times, Oct. 7].

That scene was repeated all across the nation, wherever William Booth preached. "Not since the visit of Dwight L. Moody," stated the newspapers in the largest cities, "have such audiences filled every inch of space in our auditoriums." "No buildings," wrote General Booth to his friend John Cory, "that we have been able to secure, have been large enough for the Sunday and evening attendances. In some places the fights outside for admission have been really dangerous, limbs having been fractured and lives been endangered by the eagerness of the people to get in" [*Begbie*, II: 247]. Would it be irreverent to suggest that William Booth in his day was as popular as Elvis Presley or the Beatles in theirs?

Chapter Twenty

What was there still about this remarkable man that so captivated the American public? The novelty of the Salvation Army—with its unique dual mission of spiritual and social reclamation—was partly an answer. But, mainly, it was the personality and achievement of the general himself, his distinctive appearance and preaching style, which so intrigued people. They had gotten a taste of his charm, and his passion, when he had visited a few years ago and, if they hadn't, they were compelled this time to do so when they read, in nearly all American newspapers, descriptions of his style and person. When local reporters failed to supply the incentive, it was generously supplied to local newspapers by English journalists. In fact, one of the most popular descriptions of William Booth was written by the well-known editor of *T.P.'s Weekly* and was carried by many American newspapers at the time of his arrival:

"It is impossible to see General Booth for a moment and ever forget him, for he has one of the most striking faces I have ever seen. It is, as 'twere, drawn on granite by a pencil of steel. The rigidity, the clearness, the firmness of the lines, make it difficult to believe that it is flesh and blood, and not the hardness, the coldness, and impenetrability of stone. The face is thin, long, hatchet-shaped, and yet the lines are fine and even noble. The nose—more like the beak of an eagle than the nose of an ordinary man— juts out in a promontory. It is as large and commanding a nose as that of Wellington [Arthur Wellesley, first Duke of Wellington and Prime Minister of England] but it is finer in cut and in shape. Then there is the long, slightly shaggy beard, the fine, full head of hair; the high and prominent cheek bones; the mouth finely curved, regular, firm-set, all produce the impression of a man with tremendous power of will, of command, and of infectious enthusiasm. And the body, long, thin, without an ounce of superfluous flesh, almost gaunt, increases the impression of one of those beings whose energies are exhaustless because the splendid endurance of nature has never been dulled by the self-indulgences of the ordinary man.

"The picture I have attempted to give suggests a greater severity of expression than would be accurate. That was not the impression made upon me. Tremendous fire—force of character—great power of command—occasionally power of stern severity—all these things must be in the man who has been able to keep together this vast Army of men and women in the bond of an iron discipline for so many years. But, if I misjudge him not, there is much softness in this man's heart and temperament.

CHARGED WITH PURPOSE

"Indeed, if there had not been, how could he have taken up that work which so many of the churches had neglected—the work of saving, not the fashionable lady nor the paunchy shopkeeper, nor even the workingman in Sunday broadcloth, but the ragged, the hungry, the outcast, the convict, the Magdalen? The soft light in the eyes of General Booth, the serenity of the expression, the outlook as of a benign wonder and pity for the world—all these things produced a favorable impression upon me of the man's inner life. After all, every face is beautiful, 'charged with purpose,' to use Mr. Gladstone's famous phrase, and the face of General Booth is indeed charged with purpose . . .

"I am told that General Booth has but one weakness left—the love of tea, which means that throughout his life, and in a land and age of self-indulgence, of almost brutish over-eating and over-drinking, this man has kept white and pure and undefiled the fine temple of his body, and is thus, in old age, the same lithe, fiery, untrammeled, and restless spirit of his youth. With the spiritual gospel which General Booth preaches I have naught here to do, but as a living embodiment of the gospel of simplicity, purity, sanity, sobriety, I regard him as one of the most inspiring teachers of our time."

It is little wonder then that, given such fulsome publicity, so many Americans crammed themselves into various auditoriums to experience for themselves what others had told them would be an unforgettable evening. And what they saw, for the most part, was what the journalists said he was: a commanding personality, a speaker with fire and passion, whose life history almost defied belief.

A TOUCH OF MEGALOMANIA

One fact was now becoming obvious: William Booth was getting old. And with age many of his temperamental traits and idiosyncrasies were accentuated—or, shall we say, became more publicly prominent. He had always been a man of exacting demands, fussy eating habits, with an imperious manner, which sometimes tended to offend. Now, on this trip in his seventy-third year, he was perhaps getting more crotchety and was letting his guard down more often in public—revealing a temperament, and a touch of megalomania, which took some people by surprise but which further endeared him to the public as exhibiting that touch of eccentricity which all great men are supposed to possess.

When he was speaking, for example, the general could no longer tolerate the least disturbance from the audience: the doors were barred, and no person was allowed in or out during his sermon or lecture. Lawley was there, of course, to inspect each auditorium and ensure that the windows were curtained so that no light beams distracted him; and, especially to see that no babies were admitted. The last of these disturbing influences had been prohibited during William Booth's previous visit to Canada.

"Make Your Choice"

"When we reached the church [at Peterborough]," Lawley wrote, "where the afternoon meeting was to be held, if there was one pram in the churchyard there were 50, to say nothing of the little folk holding their mothers' skirts. The little dears chirruped from gallery to gallery; their mothers danced and bounced them up and down, to keep them from crying. The general made a valiant attempt, but for him to talk with that moving picture before his eyes was an agony.

"He felt he lost the meeting and was much distressed. When we got alone, he said, 'Now, Lawley, we've been coming up to this for a long time. Make your choice. You shall have babies or me.' On the spot we settled the familiar announcement—'Children with or without parents are not permitted.'" And so it was to be throughout his visit.

A Team Effort

In Toledo a bat got into the hall where the general was speaking and flew round and round in terror of the electric lights. Frederick Cox, his secretary, was sitting behind the general, and was getting quite nervous at his signs of agitation. The general's daughter, Emma, well-known for her little penciled messages during meetings, passed to Cox a scribbled note: "Cox, join your faith with mine, and pray that bat out of the building." Cox lifted his heart to God, and in that moment the bat made a mad dash for an open door, and swept out of the hall. Two pairs of eyes met in mutual acknowledgment as the consul murmured "Hallelujah." [*He Was There!* p. 60]

If someone was whispering, or rustling the program, or otherwise annoying him, William Booth would publicly reprimand them, much to their embarrassment, but often to the delight of the audience because it further endowed him with a sense of individuality and humanity.

A Burden to Bear

For his attendants, however, and especially for his private secretary, Brigadier Fred Cox, William Booth's obsessions could be burdensome, even if sometimes humorous. As Cox has shown in his diary (later published as *He Was There*, 1949), and as many others have verified, General Booth had always been a man of methods but now importunately so. He demanded punctuality, deplored unfilled time, pooh-poohed hobbies (why do a crossword puzzle when one could be preparing a sermon), had no time for casual conversation and preferred to talk rather than listen.

Arriving at a train station with only a minute or two to spare ("What will people think if they see me idling?" asked William Booth), Cox would see the general to his railway carriage, very often a private carriage placed at his disposal by the railway company. On entering General Booth would select a seat with its back to the engine, "off the wheels (to relieve from vibration), preferring, however, the side upon which he got the light on his left, so avoiding shadow when writing. If going on a long journey [say, from Colorado Springs to Los Angeles], he instantly removed his boots, putting on slippers, replacing his hat with a traveling cap, getting his paper case open by his side, his fountain pen, his writing pad, and all other working tools in order, and would then say, 'Now for the Guide, Cox' [meaning *The Soldier's Guide* containing portions of daily scripture].

"I would read a portion. He and I would pray—then I would open my typewriter, and for two or three hours we would work. Then his lunch—a hard-boiled egg, some cress sandwiches, and a spoonful of rice pudding, or bread and butter pudding with a few currants or raisins on it, a slice of cheese—then a cup of tea, and an hour's rest, during which the windows would be darkened. Then up and work once more until we got to the journey's end" [*He Was There*, p. 42].

At one point in his diary, Fred Cox made a list of what he called his "daily duties." "Ultimately," writes his biographer, "the list numbered nearly two hundred items—enough to terrify any would-be successor." Here are a few of these, some tinged with his irrepressible sense of humor:

- Answer bell when rung, whether night or day.
- Prevent streaks of light at windows.
- Carbonate of soda must be kept in pocket.
- Have comb in pocket for use at any moment.
- In combing hair, never scratch the scalp. "Comb the hair, not the head!"
- Never allow the handicapped, children, or press on front seat.
- Looking glasses must always be covered up in bedrooms.
- Toast must always be crisp and hot.
- Tea should be strong, and served with boiling hot milk.
- If the general says a thing is so, it is so—never mind what your opinion may be on the matter! [Ibid, pp. 38-39].

NEEDS AND WANTS

Such were William Booth's needs (and demands), especially on a long trip such as this, that a cartload of luggage ("18 pieces" says Cox) had to be transported to and from each lodging. And Cox, ever inventive, had a special overcoat made containing as many as 43 pockets ("ever a wonder to children and of anxiety to [my] tailor"), each with a definite purpose—travel tickets, handkerchiefs, lozenges, bicarbonate of soda, paper fasteners, a railway carriage door key, even a spare denture, to name but a few—the general's needs were always anticipated.

Cox confided to his wife that "now my whole time is with the g., day and night. I never leave him, save and only when I run out to get shaved. When he sleeps I must be near to watch and guard; when he wakes I must be handy to answer his call; when he is on the platform I must be behind him or beside him; when he rides to and from the station I must accompany. You know my little electric bell? Well, I am never further from him than the sound of that bell."

SLEEPING ARRANGEMENTS

The reference to "that bell" is quite fascinating. It was a traveling essential, going everywhere William Booth did, along with an odd assortment of other devices. J. Evan Smith, a later private secretary, tells of the general's nightly rituals in a little book called *Booth the Beloved* (1949). "One essential of our traveling equipment was folds of black cloth and drawing pins. The general was a very light sleeper, and upon arriving at a lodging it was necessary to adjust things in the bedroom in such a way as would be conducive to comfort and rest. The slightest chink of light streaming through the window at dawn would be sufficient to wake the general, so it was necessary to cover the window with this black material and effectively darken the room. Sometimes this presented a real difficulty. I did not want to make any more fuss than necessary by disturbing the host or hostess, and so would get a chair, or, if in a large mansion where windows were high and wide, I would have to clamber upon a table or dresser, stretching up to fix the drawing pins, seeing to it that every little glimmer of light was eliminated . . . The bed would then be made up [Booth carried his own bedclothes and used them in some places] and the pillows suitably fixed, placed back to the window, including the fixing of the portable electric bell push."

INFINITE PATIENCE

"Fixing the portable electric bell" meant stringing a wire from the general's bedroom to that of his secretary (always next door), attaching the "push" (button) to the general's bed, so that at any time of the night he could call for help—for example, with transcribing his thoughts. His ideas most often came to him at night when he was so restless. "To realize something of Cox's devoted loyalty to his leader," writes his son, "one must appreciate that his most intimate contacts with him were, often, just at those times when the old man was played out—at the conclusion of gigantic meetings in which the general had exhausted his physical and nervous resources—meetings in which he would preach for an hour and more at a time, gripping the mighty crowds. After such meetings sleep did not come easily, and at these times the afflictions and sorrows of mankind bore in upon him with special intensity. So it was often a weary, suffering old man, with frayed nerves and all the irritability born of chronic indigestion, with whom Cox had to deal."

UNCONVENTIONAL DIET

Sometimes, of course, the hosts and hostesses with whom William Booth stayed, or the hotel staffs who tended to him, also had to deal with his eccentric habits, especially as regards food. General Booth was, as is well known, for most of his life a vegetarian, eating neither fish, meat nor fowl, not even vegetables cooked with fat. "His diet," stated a writer in *The Indiana Progress*, "is solely upon cereals, boiled rice being largely his sustenance. He occasionally eats rice for breakfast, dinner and supper and then enters upon the same diet next day." He was a vegetarian, it was said, "not merely because he believes that mankind—Adam and Eve of the Bible—were vegetarians, but because, after a long practical trial, he finds himself far younger than his years while the mortal parts of most men, who laugh at what they call his crankiness, are like John Brown's body—a-moldering in the grave."

William Booth was, therefore, often a difficult guest to please. He could not, for example, tolerate the noise of children and, if there were any, they had to be kept quiet for the duration of his stay. "Needless to say," wrote one disgruntled hostess, "we had to turn all the chimes off our clock in the hall, as the secretary said it was 'enough to awaken the saints in heaven.' Nearly all our doors had to be pasted with dusters to prevent them banging, and orders were sent down to 'shut up the dog.'"

As for the poor maids (every one of whom William Booth called "Mary"), they suffered great confusion when the general would one morning send back his toast because it was "too thick" and the very next morning send it back because it was "too thin." The general's favorite drink, as we know, was strong tea, "diluted with plenty of boiled milk," and this, he insisted, should be served very hot. If less than scalding he would not complain to the hostess but turn to the maid, standing by, and, with his hand encircling the cup, call out in his deepest tones, "Mary, Mary, I like my tea as I like my religion—*hot, very hot.*"

INSTRUCTIONS TO HOSTS

When staying with private families (generally very well-to-do socialites), the following letter always preceded him:

Dear Friend,

I am informed that you have very kindly undertaken to entertain General Booth during his visit to your town, and, as his requirements are somewhat unusual—though very simple—we feel sure you will welcome the information as to his needs which we have the pleasure to give below.

The general does not take fish, flesh or fowl in any shape or form.

The following will be all he desires:

Tea, about 4:30: Strong Ceylon tea, boiling hot milk, white bread, dry toast and butter, with the addition of a few fried potatoes (or mushrooms, if convenient).

In making the toast, the bread should be cut tolerably thin, and gradually toasted until it is both dry and crisp, and yet not too hard, and should be then immediately placed in the rack.

If staying at a hotel (as he often did in the United States), he would exasperate the staff by his insistence on the proper protocol and his policy of never leaving a tip. One report of such an occasion, now rather amusing, was carried by several newspapers in 1902.

FASTIDIOUSNESS

Kansas City *Star*: "It is said that meat has not passed the lips of General William Booth for 61 years. At the age of 12 years he became a vegetarian and his children have followed his example. At the Hotel Baltimore where the Salvation Army leader was a guest during his recent visit to this city, many stories about his gastronomic peculiarities are told. Every dish ordered had to be served in accordance with rules prescribed by the general and promulgated by his secretary. Toast had to be browned to a particular shade and "stood on end" to dry; milk had to be a certain temperature, and vegetables served in dishes of peculiar patterns. Prince Dafney, a waiter in the hotel café, was detailed by the management to look after the inner wants of the general and he says the task was the hardest he has yet undertaken.

SOCIAL PROTOCOL

" 'The general had to have everything just so,' said Prince today, "and he kept me busy planning not to displease him. His meals were served in his room and his daughter, Consul Booth-Tucker, sat at his table. In a corner of the room his private secretary was served. At every meal he would raise his hands over his head and say, 'Lord, bless the waiter.' The first time he said it I smiled and waited for a tip, for I had worked hard to please him, but after the blessing he apparently forgot me. After that whenever he blessed me I just looked the other way.

"In the culinary department the general's orders were not appreciated. The chefs are not used to cooking for vegetarians. Three times a day they were called upon to serve three orders, all exactly the same. For breakfast the triple order called for thin dry toast, soft-boiled eggs, hot rolls, French bread and fresh butter, hot milk, cold cream. For dinner the bill of fare was tomato soup, large mushrooms on toast, cabbage, mashed potatoes, boiled macaroni, French bread and fresh butter, cheese wafers, lemon ice cream and hot milk. For supper, boiled Spanish onions, with cream sauce, steamed rice, French bread and fresh butter, hot milk and chocolate were served.

"General Booth invariably uses his own bed covering. When he entered his bedchamber his first order was that the bed be stripped of its costly linen and woolen coverings. The chambermaid who obeyed the summons could not at first understand what was expected of her. The general explained. When she had performed the task the saver of souls raised his hands and solemnly said, 'Lord, bless the maid.' "

A LASTING IMPRESSION

No doubt many similar stories remained untold, or were circulated with amusement at private dinner parties. William Booth, both as private and public person, would not be forgotten in America for many years to come. Although he was growing frail, had many idiosyncrasies, and ruffled many feathers, he was still a power to be reckoned with. He was still a passionate and persuasive preacher with amazing stamina, and, as Harold Begbie writes, "the same earnestness, the same humanity, the same simplicity of soul which characterized his youthful preaching in Nottingham [England] streets."

Chapter Twenty-One

In 1902, William Booth began the main part of his American tour in Buffalo, New York, on November 8 and traveled along the southern shore of Lake Erie, stopping at Conneaut, Ohio (where "the Opera House was filled to the last chair"), southeast to Columbus and then north to Detroit, Toledo and west again to Chicago. In that city, whose nearly 30 corps combined to produce one of the largest Salvationist congregations in the nation, General Booth again spent a week at what they called a Chicago field congress. "Every hour of all the crowded week had been legislated for. Sixteen public meetings, besides interviews, correspondence and business galore. Long prayer meetings, which would surely have taxed the strength of younger men than our general, had been reveled in, and seldom could our leader be persuaded to leave the bridge of action, however late the hour, before the penitent-form had been several times filled with anxious seekers, yielding to the Spirit's call" [*War Cry*, Dec. 13].

For the most part, barring minor exceptions, the receptions, the public adulation, and William Booth's sermons and lectures were very similar—and similarly appreciated—to what they were five years earlier. In almost every newspaper the description went something like this: "The largest crowd that ever filled the First Methodist Episcopal Church sat motionless and spellbound for an hour and 35 minutes last night while an aged, white-bearded man, tremulous and feeble as he rose, poured forth in ringing tones a volume of oratory such as has been seldom heard in this city. As he talked, he seemed to grow years younger, and, fired by the enthusiasm of his subject, sent his deep bass voice straight into the heart of every listener" [*Duluth News*, Nov. 28].

"Keep the Pot Boiling"

By 1902, The Salvation Army had become a well-respected organization, and its social-welfare efforts an entrenched feature of American life.

Thus, at around Christmas time, when William Booth was in Los Angeles, it was the Army's nationwide "Keep the Pot Boiling" appeal and its free dinners for the poor that engaged the public's attention. Emma Booth-Tucker's name was associated most frequently with that effort: she assisted at the Christmas dinner in San Francisco, while her husband, Frederick, looked after the one in New York which treated 12,500 people to a Christmas dinner. It was becoming a cherished American tradition and was publicized along the following lines in many American newspapers at that season.

BASKETS AND BLESSINGS

"Each year so long as I live and the Christmas time comes again I shall think of Consul Emma Booth-Tucker of the Salvation Army distributing baskets and blessings to the poor and lowly on December 25. In connection with that scene somehow always comes to me the thought of the redemption of the race and of Jesus of Nazareth feeding the 5,000 hungry ones with miraculous loaves and fishes, albeit the loaves and fishes Mrs. Booth-Tucker dispenses are not the least miraculous, and, what is more, not a few of them are provided by wealthy and kindly men and women of the Hebrew faith. It is something that could hardly happen outside of the United States—Jews aiding generously to provide in honor of the birthday of the Founder of the Christian faith to be distributed by the heads of the Salvation Army to 25,000 hungry people of all races, all religions and many of no religion at all.

"In the largest cities of the Union this annual Salvation Army Christmas dinner has its place. For weeks before the 25th of December at street corners in the most crowded thoroughfares are earthenware pots hung upon cross sticks in imitation of gypsy cooking pots. A wire netting is over each so not to tempt weak brethren to snatch its contents. The meshes of the netting are large enough to permit bank notes and all sizes of silver coins being slipped within them. Upon a placard above the pot are inscribed the words, 'Keep the Pot Boiling.' A gentle, blue-uniformed sister in a scoop bonnet stands guard over the pot, or sometimes in the busiest or toughest localities it may be two Salvation Army soldiers. This is the Army's unique method of appealing to the public to help it give a dinner to from 10,000 to 30,000 hungry persons on Christmas day . . .

BLESSING, POWER AND MAGIC

"In New York no building except Madison Square Garden is large enough to hold the Salvation Army diners and guests. It is there Mrs. Emma Booth-Tucker may be found on Christmas, when she is not out of the city on Army affairs. Weeks before Christmas morning Army soldiers have been preparing for these dinners. The cooked feast is served in the evening. In the early part of the day baskets of eatables, uncooked, are distributed to the just and the unjust. A stream of humanity that begins to gather by 8 o'clock pours into one door and passes out the opposite one, each person carrying a basket containing food ample for four persons—a fowl, vegetables, fruit and some cake or candy . . .

FOUR THOUSAND BASKETS

"In the center of the great enclosure stand usually Commander and Mrs. Booth-Tucker and their aides. There seems a radiant atmosphere about the spot where Emma Booth-Tucker stands. Those 4,000 baskets are largely delivered to the recipients with her own hands. Long, delicate, frail looking hands they are, yet there are blessing and power and magic in their touch. This tall, slight woman with the golden brown hair looks so fragile that a wind might blow her away, yet for three hours she stands and deals out dinners and blessings.

"As she gives out the baskets she has a good word for each person, and her voice is musical and thrilling. To one she murmurs 'Merry Christmas,' to another 'Happy New Year,' to another, an old and trembling woman, 'God bless you, mother!' Tears are in the old woman's eyes as she passes on with her precious Christmas dinner. Then the radiant soul that blessed her gives a basket to the next, the toughest, most battered looking wreck in all that motley throng, and tells him God loves him" [Esther E. Cullen].

Such stories—and the actual work of which they spoke—were what, in 1902, made William Booth's reception in America so cordial.

For he, as did his daughter Emma, epitomized the essence of Salvationism, and Americans revered him for it. Indeed, the word "venerable" was most often used to describe him, which he thoroughly liked, even though it was as often accompanied by "old man," which he did not like at all.

BELOW THE MASON-DIXON

As much as he loved re-visiting America's major cities, seeing familiar faces and getting to his soldiers once again, William Booth was still seeking new worlds to conquer—or, in this case, new areas of the United States. The one he had not yet visited previously was the Deep South. Though the Army was only sparsely established there, he was anxious to further its mission and, even if not immediately successful in that regard, to at least experience the deep-set revival tradition of southern Americans.

And that is what he did with great satisfaction when, for the first time, he visited the cities of Chattanooga, Nashville, Memphis, Dallas, New Orleans, Mobile, Birmingham and Atlanta. "Where a few days ago we were freezing," wrote one member of the party, "now we are sweltering." Not from the weather only, but from warmth of the people who, in the thousands, packed the various halls where William Booth preached or lectured."

RED-HOT AND BOILING OVER

In Mobile, Alabama (Feb. 4-5), General Booth accepted an invitation to preach to a congregation of over 1,000 black people in the Zion Church. "A right royal reception was his," wrote the *War Cry* correspondent. Sing? I should think they did! You should have heard it! It was a thunderous volley of beautiful melody."

The *War Cry* reporter wrote: "The prayer-meeting was a red-hot, boiling-over time, and as one after the other of the penitents came forward, our friends simply went wild with enthusiasm, and clapped their hands and shouted 'Glory to God!' with all the strength, lungs, voice, and throat they possessed. It was 11:15 when I left the church, and both houses and streets in the neighborhood nearby were alive with songs of salvation, loud shoutings of 'Hallelujahs' and praises to God, which came from the souls who had just entered the Kingdom [Feb. 28, 1903].

SIMPLE, CONVINCING DRAMA

"After an evidently stereotyped opening, his speech begins to take form and color, to show the character of the man making it. Earnestness, absolute and telling, is the dominant note. The man evidently believes in himself and his work, and this work of his, according to all intelligent observers, is worth hearing about, especially when the man who has done it tells the story of his achievements.

"And now the audience stills itself and remains rapt. The silence is unbroken, save by the voice with the earnest ring in it that gathers strength with each moment until it is distinctly heard in every part of the house.

"Under the focus of thousands of eyes, the general goes on with his speech. He has none of the arts of the orator. He is singularly simple, almost awkwardly convincing, and yet dramatic withal. He sways constantly on his feet, without a gesture of any sort, until he pictures the marching hosts whom the Salvation Army has saved; then he tramps back and forth before his auditors, stopping only to make sweeping gestures with both hands. All this his hearers note until the man is almost forgotten in the story he is relating.

"It is so plain and straightforward that no one can fail to understand, and its theme so vast that its greatness alone commands attention and holds the interest of all present. Even the interest increases as the picture grows under the sound of that queer voice with the incessant earnestness. The Army—of one man—is barely to be seen in the slough of London's slums. But it grows in numbers and influence, its flags fly in every breeze, its songs resound in every country. Its few saved sinners become thousands, its good works brighten the lives of all humanity. It deserves help everywhere.

TRANSFIXED

"The audience draws a long breath and reaches out hands filled with silver to the baskets that are passing. It keeps its eyes on the figure on the stage, for a strange thing has happened—an old man, worn by long service, had developed before its eyes into a giant, a fit leader of a military organization. It seems wonderful, almost incredible, yet all this is true. Each person in the vast audience has witnessed the transformation and feels that the speaker is a wonderful man. That General Booth's hearers have listened for more than an hour without sound or movement save at long intervals astonishes them until they have time to think more quietly of what the man has said; then wonder ceases" [Feb. 9].

CHOICE PHRASES

So intrigued was the reporter by William Booth's speeches that he culled some of the general's wittiest phrases, offering them to his readers as a choice set of aphorisms:

- "If I was in a business where I could not serve God I would chuck it up and let the devil have it."

- "Every man who is not saved is under the influence of some slave or evil passion, which claims him to darkness."

- "I wonder how many wives are going to hell rather than displease their husbands, or how many husbands are going to hell rather than displease their wives."

- "People are curious about the Salvation Army because it is a success. No one ever had any curiosity about a thing that is a failure."

- "I am fond of shooting and fishing—shooting at the devil and catching sharks and whales."

- "The Salvation Army is spreading so fast that if our geographical friends don't watch we will reach the North Pole before they do."

- "When a man's watch gets out of order he doesn't take it to a blacksmith. When his heart gets out of order he must take it to God, its Maker."

- "When I was so sick my doctors said I should hunt some small country parish. I found it, and it reaches from London to Birmingham."

- "Some are interested enough in the Salvation Army to throw a dollar at it as they pass along, just as they would throw a bone to a dog."

CULTURE UNSUITED TO ARMY

Altogether the trip south was not as pleasant or profitable as General Booth had expected. He had expected to initiate discussions regarding the acquisition of land on which to establish yet another "farm colony." These did not take place and that idea was abandoned. He also saw that the Salvation Army was making but slow headway in a society where church-going—especially to churches of the revival kind—was a well-established habit and where the culture was not suited to the Army's social egalitarianism.

He therefore did not see fit to encourage much expansion in the South. The Army's work was still in its embryo stage, he reasoned, was (in his words) encountering "untold difficulties," the main one being a shortage of funds, and it was therefore not an opportune time to plan new openings or expansion. As one officer put it sometime earlier, it would require "lots of thrusting and stirring about to make a success of the South." And, in spite of William Booth's assertion that an effort would be made to "put the Army on a high plane," the future in that part of the vineyard did not look too bright.

Chapter Twenty-Two

If William Booth's tour of the South had been less gratifying than he had expected, his return to the North made him quickly forget whatever disappointments he might have harbored. For, again, Washington, D.C., restored his confidence in America's wholehearted support of his mission. On Wednesday, February 11, he was guest at a large dinner party at the Arlington Hotel hosted by his good friend, Senator Mark Hanna, a wealthy industrialist and Republican politician who had been a close friend of President McKinley (assassinated in 1901) and was now the most powerful member of the United States Senate.

Speaking of the Salvation Army, Senator Hanna said: "I have been in touch with the movement of which General Booth is the head for many years, and I am in full sympathy with it. I have observed the good results in my own city, where I have been in close contact with the efforts and consequent results, and I have also noted the outcome of the work of the Army throughout the country. It is a noble work, being conducted conscientiously and faithfully by a devoted band. I am glad to cooperate with them in every way, and I am glad to pay the tribute of my esteem and consideration to the man who is at the head of the movement" [*NY Times*, Feb. 12, 1903].

Among those invited were the elite of American politicians—every conspicuous figure in the public life of the capital was present, including the vice-president, the speaker, and members of the Supreme Court, the Cabinet, the Senate, and the House—enough to buoy up General Booth's sagging spirits. "Quite a number of influential men gathered around the beautifully decorated table," he wrote in his journal, "and partook of the dainties set before them, and when they had well eaten and the cigars had been handed round [to which he took no exception!], Mr. Hanna introduced me with a few very hearty and appropriate words of recommendation respecting myself personally and the work in general.

"I talked for an hour, got a little confused here and there, and left unsaid some of the more important things I wanted to say. Still I talked freely out of my heart, and pleaded hard for my poor people. Whatever my own opinion was of my performance (and it was not a very high one, indeed quite the contrary), the views entertained respecting it by every individual present, expressed in the frankest manner either in the speeches made after I sat down or at the final handshake, were most favorable to the Army, and of deepest sympathy for its continued and increased success" [*Begbie*, II: 254].

OVERCAME, DISARMED, CAPTURED

William Booth's opinion of his poor performance, though obviously overstated, had good reason. He was tired, having arrived late from Atlanta, had not been able to sleep that afternoon, and was ill at ease in the company of so many prominent people who, with their cigars and political talk, were not his kind. But, as he warmed to his subject, he gained confidence and finally rose to the occasion. Here is how one of the participants, the Honorable Henry Macfarland, described it:

"When General Booth arose [to speak], he looked tired and ill at ease. His voice was husky from the effort of the many speeches of his tour, and he spoke in low tones. His first few sentences made no impression, except, possibly, to add to the general feeling of coldness. Senator Hanna's face showed fear of failure.

"Suddenly one of the senators at the extreme right said, 'Louder!' This gave the old general just the shock he needed. He threw up his head and straightened out his form like an old lion suddenly roused to action. Snapping back, 'Oh, I can shout if necessary!' he raised his voice so that it could be heard all through the banquet suite. He spoke possibly an hour, continually gripping, more and more, first the head then the heart of his audience.

"It was a memorable study to watch those who had never heard him before, and he gradually overcame their indifference, disarmed their criticism, and captured their attention, and, finally, admiration. His hearers were the hardest men in the country to affect by speaking. All of them were familiar with all the arts and tricks of every form of public speaking—in courts, in Congress, on the stump. No company of the same number could have been assembled in their country at that time including more public speakers of experience and success. Senator Hanna could not have selected for the purpose a more formidable company of men.

EARNEST AND SINCERE

"The Salvationist chief took them captive without them knowing how. In form General Booth's speech was not eloquent any more than his voice, which, though strong, was rough and harsh. In truth, the speech violated all the canons of oratory but one, and that the only one that cannot be violated without failure. The canon, of course, is that which requires sincerity and earnestness. It was evident that the speaker was genuine, and it was equally evident that he was speaking of real life. But it was most evident that he was speaking, as was said of Whitefield [George Whitefield, evangelist and a founder of Methodism] 'like a dying man to dying men,' without thought of the outward rank or popular reputation of those to whom he spoke.

MOVED TO TEARS

"When General Booth sat down he had completely changed the atmosphere of the occasion, and the minds of all the men before him. Senator Hanna, rising to speak, searched in all his pockets for a handkerchief, and finding none, picked up his napkin from the table and wiped tears from his cheeks. He was not the only man who had not been able to repress the tears. All were greatly moved, each according to his temperament. What Senator Hanna then said was very different from what he said in his introduction. But no words could equal the tribute of tears" [*The Chicago Continent*, Feb.15, 2003].

CHANGE OF MIND

Many others—mainly senators—were also touched by William Booth's vivid depiction of the Army's work; one might say many were "converted" by his passion and personality. One of these, Senator Hoar of Massachusetts, remarked:

"I confess that I labored under a total misapprehension of the Salvation Army in the past. Indeed, when I have seen the parades and meetings on the corners of the streets, I admit to having felt like bidding them fulfill their Master's command to go to their closets and shut their door and pray to the Father in secret. But, after hearing General Booth this evening, I can clearly see what a narrow and perverted judgment I had formed, and how completely I have been mistaken in regard to their work.

"I have listened with the deepest interest to the eloquent story of the founder of this remarkable movement. I thank you, Senator Hanna, for the opportunity afforded me. It has carried me back to the times of the apostles, and to the noblest records of the martyrs and pilgrims of old. It seems to me as though we had been in telepathic communication with those heroes of bygone days. It will afford me pleasure henceforth to do anything within my power to assist those consecrated people in their noble work" [*War Cry*, March 7, 1903].

DINING WITH ROOSEVELT

Senator Hanna's banquet, however, was, as Harold Begbie puts it, "only a prelude to other important events," all no doubt owing much to the senator's powerful influence. On the following day, February 12, General Booth, with his son-in-law, Frederick Booth-Tucker, was invited to lunch with President Theodore Roosevelt, who had become president on the death of William McKinley in 1901 and was, when William Booth had last been in Washington, preparing his troops for an invasion of Cuba. "The President takes the liveliest interest in the work of the Salvation Army," stated the *NY Times*, "knowing personally of the results achieved by it, particularly in the large cities" [Feb. 12]. That he indeed did so is substantiated by William Booth himself:

"We were ushered in the most informal manner, and on entering found Mr. Hay, Secretary for Foreign Affairs; Mr. Root, Secretary for War; and Mr. Hitchcock, Secretary for the Interior. After introduction to these gentlemen, I had a nice chat with them. We were shortly after joined by another gentleman much interested in some kind of slum settlement in New York.

John Singer Sargent

"The President then entered, shaking hands all around in the cheeriest manner. Mr. Roosevelt was accompanied by a Mr. Sargent, who, I was afterwards given to understand, has a worldwide reputation as a portrait painter. [This would have been John Singer Sargent—Ed.]

"During the conversation at dinner I heard it stated that this artist was present for the purpose of painting a likeness of the President; Mr. Roosevelt remarking that he had been through all the rooms at the White House that had been proposed for the sitting, and had not found one suitable, until in coming down the stairs to lunch Mr. Sargent had stopped him at a certain point, and declared that that was just the very place and position that would be suitable to his task.

"We were soon seated and busy with the food; conversation never flagged for a moment, the president having a long way the lion's share of the talking. All manner of things were chatted about, some of them weighty, and some of very much lighter importance, at least so they appeared to me. After a little while the president, who had seated me at his side, turned to me and entered into a conversation on the character of our work. He seemed very interested in our criminal operations, the efforts for the rescue of poor lost women, and the colonization of land.

"Unfortunately some business matter called his attention off, and he turned aside to write a memorandum and then something came up with the Venezuela affair, which Mr. Hay informed him was he believed near a hopeful settlement, and so the talk drifted on until the repast was ended.

"The President rose, assured me of the pleasure it had afforded him to meet me, wished me good luck, and we all went our way" [*Begbie*, II: 259].

A Remarkable Experience

And, finally, to culminate the official recognition of the Army's founder, on February 13 General Booth was again asked to open the daily session of the United States Senate in prayer (See Appendix B). "The Senate," states the *NY Times*, "was crowded today as it has not been since the opening day of the session. Nearly all the senators were on the floor; many members of the House were present, while the sides of the chamber were lined with employees. The galleries were filled, many visitors standing in the aisles. The attraction was General William Booth of the Salvation Army . . ."

Again William Booth records the moment in his diary:

"In company with Senator Hanna and the Commander [Booth-Tucker], we drove to the Capitol for the performance of the opening of the Senate with prayer, to which I had been invited.

"I had not looked forward to this affair as being of any importance, but it certainly turned out to be one of the most interesting if not remarkable incidents of my life . . .

A SUDDEN STILLNESS

"The House was unusually crowded, some people saying that the galleries had not been so packed for 30 years, while all agreed that no such assemblage had taken place during this session; and more remarkable than the crowd in the gallery was the attendance of the senators themselves; every man seemed to be in his place, and when the vice-president made the usual sign and I was conducted to the chair he usually occupied, a sudden stillness fell upon the assembly. Every head, they afterwards told me, was reverently bowed, while I asked God's blessing on the men chosen for so important a share in the direction of the destinies of this great nation, and for wisdom and strength to do the work to the divine satisfaction, and for the highest well being of those concerned.

FEELING ANXIETY

"I must confess to feeling beforehand some little anxiety as to the way I should be able to discharge this duty. While desirous, as I hope I ever am when approaching the mercy-seat, to speak to God regardless of the feelings with which my performance may be regarded by those around me, I was still anxious that the few sentences I had the opportunity of speaking and which I knew would be so closely criticized, and so widely circulated, should carry with them useful lessons and inspire profitable feelings.

"I had a dim recollection that three minutes was allowed for the function, but although I asked Senator Hanna and a few others, including the chaplain, I could get no definite pronouncement on the subject, the general opinion being, I fancy, as I learned afterwards was the case—that I should not be likely to infringe on the decorum of the House by taking any unusual liberty in this direction.

SPIRIT-FILLED

"As I stood there a world of feeling came rushing upon me; memories of past struggles, influences of the kind things said about myself and my doings, and the possibilities of the future, seemed all to come in upon me. God helped me as I lifted up my heart to Him, and he gave me words that I believe not only reached His ear, but the hearts of many present.

"I exceeded three minutes, but I did not go far beyond six—and I do not think that any one has intimated that I went too far. A good many would have liked me to have gone further!

"A motion was afterwards passed ordering that the words of the prayer be entered in the records of the House, and suspending the standing order referring to the presence of strangers in the house. Then for an hour I remained on the floor of the chamber, during which time I suppose I shook hands with every important personage present" [*Begbie*, II: 262].

Chapter Twenty-Three

To say that the Washington reception—the meeting with President Roosevelt and the honor of praying in the Senate—was the climax of William Booth's visit would be an acceptable statement. But, to suggest that the remainder of his visit—the Spirit-filled meetings in Philadelphia, Worcester, Boston and New York—was an anti-climax would be a gross misrepresentation of the truth.

POSITIVELY MAGNETIC

In Boston, for example, 3,000 people attended each of his Sunday meetings and almost 200 people responded to his invitation to seek salvation. "Every conceivable element of the city's life seemed represented in the audience," stated the *War Cry*; "there were many, no doubt, who believed they already knew a good deal about the Army, and there were not a few who came of a legitimate enough curiosity to see and hear the world-famed leader of the organization, but from the moment the general entered upon his theme they were one and all alike caught up and carried out of themselves in a very abandon of enthusiasm.

"The general himself was simply superlative: in his droll sallies of humor, his flashing lances of wit, his poignant appeals to pathos, his bold presentation of fact, his relentless arraignment of wrong-doing, his passionate championship of the lost, his proud devotion to his own people—in each and all he swayed his audience with an influence that was positively magnetic" [March 14, 1903].

After taking a few days to rest, and attend to business, General Booth concluded his tour with a week's campaign in New York. On Sunday, March 1, he conducted three rousing meetings, as here described by the *New York Daily Tribune*:

"After 20 weeks of travel and speech making in 52 cities, General Booth, of the Salvation Army, closed the evangelistic feature of his visit to this country yesterday by speaking at three meetings in the morning,

afternoon and evening, at the Academy of Music, Fourteenth Street and
Irving Place. The morning meeting opened with music by the band of
the Salvation Army headquarters. One hundred division officers were
seated on the platform, and in the empty orchestra enclosure was,
draped in red, the 'mercy seat,' and a dozen missionaries in the New
York corps of the Army.

FASTING AND DANCING

"Soon after beginning his address the general attacked the 'sin of
overeating.'

"'I have discovered that some people here eat as many as seven
times a day,' he said. 'All that is unnecessary. It means pressure on an
overstocked stomach, and the Spirit doesn't get a chance. Fast one day,
and take only bread and a little water. I told the people in the little village where I lived once the reason they had difficulty to rise up and
shout for joy in their salvation was because it was a serious affair with
a shoulder of mutton and a pork pie on their stomachs.'

"'People come to the quarters of the army and see our sisters and
brothers dancing; they are shocked. Is this religion? They ask. Certainly.
Why should the devil have all the dancing, I'd like to know? I expect to
go on dancing through all eternity. It is a great deal better than to go and
sit in a place like a lot of mummies in a pyramid in Egypt.'

SIMON AND PAUL

"Then he told of the imprisonment of Simon and Paul in a dungeon. As
he expressed it, he was 'putting a little flesh and blood on the bones.' He
said:

'It is about 11 o'clock at night when Paul wakes up from a doze.
'Simon,' he says, 'how do you feel?'
'I feel as if the Spirit of the Lord was rising in me,' says Simon.
'Good,' replied Paul. 'Let's sing.'
'And they sing until the Almighty looks down on them, and answers
with an amen and an earthquake.
'The jailer gets into his pants quicker that he ever did before in his
life, I guess, and runs down into the dungeon where he had put Paul and

Simon. When he sees them freed of the stocks he wants to commit suicide with his sword.

'Don't do it,' says Paul: 'wait and be saved.'

'And the jailer thinks that is pretty good advice, and he listens. Then Mrs. Jailer comes down. Then says Mr. Jailer to her:

'Ma, go upstairs and get breakfast while I wash the poor men's backs where they have been lashed and are bleeding.'

'And then he fills Paul and Simon full of hot coffee and new laid eggs until they can eat no more, although he had vowed to give them nothing but bread and water. And Paul and Simon convert Mr. and Mrs. Jailer and all the little jailers and a great many other people.'

"The general was followed by Colonel Lawley. Twenty-eight men and women from the audience went to the 'mercy seat.' Many of the men registered for enrollment in the Army" [March 2].

INJURY AND FATIGUE

His wit was robust, his delivery engaging; but, in truth, William Booth was now a very tired man. And the fact that, on Tuesday, he tripped on the steps of the national headquarters in New York and injured his knee, only added to his fatigue.

"The accident," he writes to Bramwell, "came at a very unfortunate moment, and at the onset it looked like spoiling the closing chapter of the campaign. But God is good. I was favored with the services of one of the most skillful and experienced surgeons in New York. He put my leg into starch, and then into a plaster of paris jacket. And by dint of resolution, and the supporting Spirit of my Heavenly Father, I went through the last meeting with apparent satisfaction to everybody about me, and some little comfort to myself. It was a great effort" [*Railton*, General Booth, p. 100].

The meeting to which Booth refers was his "Farewell to America" at the Metropolitan Opera House. "The Hall," he wrote, "is one of the finest and most imposing I ever spoke in. Three tiers of boxes all around filled with the swell class of people in whom you are so much interested, with two galleries beyond. It called for some little courage to rise up with my walking stick to steady me; but God helped me through. I hung my stick on the rail, and balanced myself on my feet, and talked the straightest truth I could command for an hour and 20 minutes" [Ibid].

As he left the Opera House, however, "his strength seemed to leave him, and he had to be assisted to a chair and carried to the automobile in which he was to lead a midnight torchlight parade down Broadway" [*NY Times, March 4*]. The vehicle had only gone a few feet when it stopped, and the chauffeur spent almost 20 minutes tinkering with the motor. It then proceeded "at a snail's pace" for a short distance and stopped again. Several sturdy male Salvationists seized the recalcitrant vehicle and propelled it a little distance before the general finally abandoned it and took a seat in a carry-all [small car with sideways seats] in which he traveled to the Army's headquarters where, "shivering in the chilly night air," he reviewed the parade.

THE CONSUMMATE SOLDIER

Six divisions of Salvationists, each with its own band, and with 1,500 torches blazing, filed down Broadway. "At every street corner were set great fires of red, and Broadway, from Thirty-third Street to Fourteenth, was aglow. In Madison and Union Squares there were set pieces of pyrotechnics, messages of farewell to the General. Accompanied by his daughter and other officers of the Army, General Booth stood on the balcony in front of the headquarters building when the marchers arrived. As the divisions drew up they took their places in front and the bands merged and played together, 'God Be With You Till We Meet Again,' and the people sang. General Booth, clinging to the railing in front, stood in the glare of a calcium light, hat in hand, despite the cold night air, and bowed continually for several minutes to the assembled Salvationists" [Ibid]. In spite of the cold, in spite of his pain, William Booth, as always, endured hardship as the consummate soldier he was.

Before he returned home, William Booth wrote to his son Bramwell these prophetic words: "Depend upon it, the United States is destined to be such a nation for population, power, intelligence, wealth, and energy as the sun has ever looked down upon." And somewhat later he wrote: "Then, as passing through an almost uninterrupted chain of thriving and influential cities, reaching from New York to San Francisco, from Chicago to New Orleans, I have gazed upon their thronged thoroughfares, making ever-increasing inroads upon even the desert and arid portions of the West. I have pictured to myself the well-nigh hundred million of her present population multiplied by two, by three, by four in the not distant future, and from this standpoint alone I cannot fail to grasp something of the mighty destiny that must await the youngest of nations in shaping the future counsels of the world" [*War Cry*, March 7, 1903].

AMERICA'S DARK SIDE

Yet, he noted with sadness, even now "a dark side to the American picture." Its large bustling cities were already infested with crime and its slums were beginning to equal any he had known in London. "Oh, what a sea of misery, present and future, is here! It must be compassionated, I am sure, by the great Father, wept over by the Savior, and lamented by the angels of heaven. It is a dark side to the American picture" [Ibid].

His sadness was softened only by the fact that he believed this was a field especially suited to the Army's special mission, by the fact that the Army "is exactly the kind of agency to deal with this ocean of sin and woe. God has called her to this special undertaking. She has a heart for the work. She loves the business. She has wonderful facilities for fitting herself to the peculiar condition and character of every people that requires her aid. [And] America is going to be no exception, and I am confident that the Salvation Army is destined for, and equal to a future victorious career which shall far exceed anything that has yet been ever dreamed of " [Ibid].

SOCIAL/EVANGELICAL SCHISM

His was an unbounded public optimism. Only a few private disappointments dampened an otherwise overwhelming enthusiasm.

In the first place, American Salvationists—the backbone of the evangelical wing—were becoming a consolidated religious community, and, though still with a downtown presence, were becoming less aggressive than they once were. In many instances, the corps units were now almost totally independent of the social institutions which were often situated nearby. This was not what William Booth had intended. All his followers, he declared, should "stick to the low places"; that was their mission. But, clearly, as the membership itself rose socially, and as the social wing assumed the responsibility of reaching the "submerged" strata of society, Salvationists began to withdraw into the confines of their "barracks" (soon to become "citadels" and "temples"). They were still, he saw, a loyal, spiritually strong people, and ever ready to witness, but were no longer simply "missionaries to the poor" but churches unto themselves.

SALVATION ARMY SHELTERS

There was so much to be proud of that any reservations might seem unwarranted. In the United States the Army had already become one of the nation's leading social benefactors and was suitably recognized as such by a grateful public. By 1903, in fact, just to cite one branch of the social work, the Army had as many as 80 shelters (often called "hotels"), the one in St. Louis offering 420 beds at five cents each and the new one in New York, called the "Braveman" (opened January, 1903) with 505 beds.

On March 1, 1903, just at the commencement of William Booth's final campaign in New York, the *Tribune* carried a full report of the new 10-story institution (15 cents a night or $1 a week) whose single most important rule was that every man who stayed must take a bath. This caused the reporter some amusement and some men great consternation, and soon caused the lodging house to be dubbed "Hotel de Bath. Patrons ride to and from their floors in elevators and act much as if they preferred the Salvation Army Hotel to any other." These hotels, plus the many Industrial Homes, Rescue Homes, salvage and slum work, guaranteed a claim on American goodwill.

FARM COLONIES

The only noticeable difference in General Booth's promotion of the social work was that the "farm colonies" so vigorously touted in 1898 were now only infrequently mentioned. The colony at Fort Amity was certainly cited as an example of success in that area of social work, but the others less so. For, in actual fact, even in 1903, it was becoming clear they were not meeting expectations, and possibly would not ever be viable enterprises. City people did not, as many critics maintained, make good farmers, but, more important, the soil, even with irrigation, was not productive and markets were not accessible. They were, it might be said, pet projects of Booth-Tucker, social-reclamation ventures which appealed to the public imagination, but support for which dwindled as Booth-Tucker's interest flagged.

And though William Booth might, as he did in one interview, proudly say that whereas the price per acre of Fort Amity was $36 when the farm was commenced and was (in 1898) worth $3,600 an acre, it would soon become clear that this was a bit of idle dreaming. For Romie, says Edward McKinley, "was sold at a small profit in 1905; Amity at a dead loss in 1909; Fort Herrick was converted briefly into an Army 'inebriates home' in 1904, then to an Army family camp in 1909; it was carried for many years at a loss on the territorial property account" [*Somebody's Brother*, p. 47].

These "colonies" in the United States were, like those planned for Canada, Australia and South Africa which never materialized at all, the one part of William Booth's *Darkest England* scheme that never really succeeded, except in a couple of instances. Though the old general was slow to recognize that fact—he still believed in his "colonization" scheme—his experience of failure in the United States and Canada eventually persuaded him to abandon the idea altogether.

COURTING THE WEALTHY

Another sobering thought, rendered as a reflection on his many public appearances, and one which William Booth noted in his letters and diaries, was the possibility that the Army (and he as general) was seen to be always courting the influential socialites and perhaps neglecting the ordinary Salvationists. He did this of necessity, he believed, because the social work simply could not survive without public support, but there was a danger, as he well recognized, that by doing so he might be consigning the evangelical wing to relative oblivion.

"As to whether we get as much real benefit out of the time and labor and ability bestowed upon feeding the poor as we should do if spent in purely spiritual work is a very difficult question to answer," he wrote, but it was, nevertheless, a very real question in his mind and the minds of many officers. And the fact that so much time had to be spent cultivating the support of influential people was also beginning to grate on some.

"On the platform were . . ." was the constant reportorial opening. "Fifty present, consisting of judges, pastors, bankers, and the like." "Mr. Hearst, of journalistic fame, Mrs. Russell Sage, Miss Gould, and a number of others of the elite of the city have taken boxes [in the theater] paying 250 dollars for a box." "General Booth welcomed by Mayor Low." And so the news items went. William Booth was, of course, very pleased to have such high-profile people on his side (though how many were simply being polite or playing politics is hard to say), but he was beginning to feel uneasy about the trend and a little tired of all the socializing.

CROSSING THE LINE?

Sometimes, in fact, the sycophantic nature of his socializing—the constant pleading for money—backfired and caused embarrassment to the Army. On several occasions, for example, the general, in his usual joking manner, would say that the Army had in their shelters more than 10,000 criminals (an exaggeration, of course) and that if the rich did not give him enough funds to carry on the work, he would turn them all loose and give them the addresses of all the rich people. This, thought some reporters, was going just a little too far, and the statement needed to be defended by Army authorities to the effect that what General Booth really meant was that, "if through lack of funds I am unable to continue my work and have to close my doors, and consequently loose those 10,000 on society, it would be very bad for these rich people."

Whatever his meaning, clearly William Booth had rich people on his mind too often. Again (how seriously is difficult to say), he stated several times his intention "to go after the millionaires of the United States and enroll them as members" of the Army. The *New York Times* (half facetiously, one suspects), thought this would be a good idea, since the qualities which made the men rich were just those needed by the Army, but, since they "were by no means the worst sinners in the community," it was unlikely they would be won in the usual Army manner and certainly would "not be captured and enrolled by means which hold them up to public attention as combustible brands to be snatched from a particularly energetic burning."

What the incident highlighted was the fact that William Booth had to tread carefully if he expected to hold the support of his well-heeled benefactors and, even though he might think their souls needed to be saved as well, he needed to underscore the social need and not press too hard on religious matters. The fact that the Army had a dual mission—religious and social—was clearly, in terms of public relations, a tricky business to promote.

GLOBAL UNIVERSITY

A final disappointment on this tour was William Booth's failed attempt to raise any interest in his proposal for a university of humanity. At his meetings in San Francisco, Washington and New York, he had made public announcements of "a plan for the establishment of an international university for the development of trained rescuers of humanity. A university of science of humanity," he said, "where men and women can be trained to reclaim depraved women, criminals and drunkards—that's what I want now. I mean a great institution, with its main establishments in London and New York, correlated with branches in Melbourne, Toronto, Berlin and Paris, from which thousands of Salvation Army workers shall be sent to the submerged masses each year, skilled in every known method of rescuing human beings from the underworld of despair."

APPEAL TO STANFORD FAMILY

It was something he had thought about earlier, and later (after his return from America) he drew up a detailed proposal for the institution. His plan was to enlist the financial support of America's wealthiest people and, to that end, he sent his daughter, Emma, back to San Francisco to "try and see Mrs. Stanford again and ask her straight out for a sum of money to carry out my wish, the establishment of a great training institution, an international university for training men and women for dealing with the sins and miseries of the submerged throughout the world."

Leland Stanford, the wealthy railway magnate, and his wife, had set aside many millions of dollars to endow a university in their son's memory in Palo Alto, California, and William Booth was hoping she (now that her husband was dead) might do the same for his university. Such support was not forthcoming, however, and the whole idea remained a dream which he would again bring to the public's attention on his next trip to America in 1907.

SHELVING THE PROJECT

Nor was it, at this time, forthcoming from any other source. In a letter to William Booth (Sept. 22, 1903), Frederick Booth-Tucker, who had been urged by the general to make his plan accessible to several wealthy people, stated that the time was simply not right. "The financial market," he said, "was weak, such that Morgan, Rockefeller and one or two other of the top men were in a state of perpetual ferment . . . It would tell against both me and the enterprise to bother them at this moment." He also noted that many other universities were already knocking at the gates of the millionaires. It is also possible that he felt that money expended on such an expensive project (some five million dollars, William Booth projected) would seriously curtail that needed for the social work. For those reasons, therefore, the university of humanity project was temporarily shelved.

THE BOOTHS IN USA

There were now three Booth children in America: Emma, Ballington and Herbert. Only the first, his dearest daughter, commanded his affection. And when we remember that just a few months later she also would be taken from him—in a terrible train crash on October 28, 1903—it must have been a blessing that Emma shared those weeks with him. She was, after all, by his side throughout the trip, had talked with him about her work ("she is indeed a marvelous conversationalist"), took his arm to support him as he walked, and, generally, was "an untold comfort and support." And though her death gave him a greater sorrow than any he had known since the death of Catherine, he was comforted by the memory of her loving devotion to both him and the Army.

In the final analysis, then, the 1902-03 visit to America was a qualified success. William Booth, of course, thought it unqualified, in spite of those few disappointments. His Salvation Army soldiers certainly did as well; and the American public, from the preponderance of editorial praise, believed likewise. And, though his body sometimes failed him, General Booth's mind never did. When asked on his return how he would describe the spiritual life of America, he gave an astute reply.

"FRIENDLY" NON-BELIEVERS

"It is very much the same as here. There is a great deal of formality among the professors of religion, and a great deal of indifference among the vast crowds—and, I think, of growing indifference—largely as a result of prosperity and of the spirit of unbelief which is rife everywhere. Yet I think their attitude towards religion is friendly . . . You can pray in an American crowd, and they won't laugh at you. You can talk at the corners of American streets, and the people will listen to you. I never once saw a sneer or heard a jeer all the time I was there. You see the difference in the newspapers . . . They drew attention to the enthusiasm and other features in conspicuous headlines, and they wrote down what happened as if the writer understood what religion is" [*Begbie*, II: 267]. The reporter for the *Daily News* who interviewed him did not ask him if he was ready to go again; but if he had, William Booth would certainly have replied, "Ready, God willing, to sail at a moment's notice." His was still a "restless heart."

General's Farewell Number.

WAR CRY

Official Gazette of the Salvation Army in the United States.

WILLIAM BOOTH, General.   Entered as New York Post Office as Second-Class Mail Matter.   EVANGELINE BOOTH, Commander.

No. 1364   120-124 W. FOURTEENTH ST., NEW YORK CITY, SATURDAY, NOVEMBER 23, 1907.   Price, 5 Cents.

Photo. Copyright by Parker, New York.

"Good-bye, General!"

(See Farewell Messages on P.

Visits 5 & 6: 1907
The Final Farewell

General William Booth, founder and head of the Salvation Army, received from the audience that packed Carnegie Hall to the doors last night what, he said, was his farewell greeting to America. The general hastened to add, however, that this announcement should not be construed as a sign of failing health, and declared that he would live as long as he could. "It has been asked," he said, "what is to become of the Salvation Army when the general passes away. I say, don't worry; the general is not dead yet."

—New York Times, Nov. 5, 1907

1907 Itinerary

First Trip

New York, March 5-8

Canada March 9-March 29

Seattle, Wash. March 30-31

Japan April 11-May 18

Second Trip

Arrived Rimouski, PQ Sept. 20

Canada Sept. 20-25

Boston, Mass. Sept. 27-30

Schenectady, NY Oct. 1

Utica, NY Oct. 2

Rochester, NY Oct. 3

Chicago, Ill. Oct. 3-10

St. Louis, Mo. Oct. 12-13

Des Moines, Iowa Oct. 15

Minneapolis, Minn. Oct. 16

Milwaukee, Wis. Oct. 17

Booth very ill: Oct. 18-23
(went to recuperate in Chicago, had to omit Cleveland)

Columbus, Ohio Oct. 25-26

Pittsburgh, Pa. Oct. 27

Washington, DC Oct. 28-29

Baltimore, Md. Oct. 30

Philadelphia, Pa. Oct. 31

New York City Nov. 2-9

Chapter Twenty-Four

"Not yet! Not yet!" William Booth would reply, with a twinkle in his eye, to the inevitable question: when would he retire from public duty? More accurately, his answer should have been, "Never!" For, as one writer put it, "the prospect of a peaceful, restful, idle old age has no allurements for him. He wants and expects to die in harness—to go about his errand of doing good to weak and sinful and suffering humanity until the burden of years overwhelms him."

Though he was nearly 78 years old, and though his sight was failing and his physical powers weakening, his passion and zeal had in no way diminished, and his mind was as sharp as ever. He would, he made it clear, not relinquish control of his Army and would continue to inspire his worldwide troops till "God called him home."

MOTOR CAR CRUSADE

The evidence of the general's boundless energy is astonishing. No sooner had he returned home from his 1902-03 tour of North America than he began planning "one of the most daring exploits of his career"— a motorcar tour of Great Britain from Land's End, in Cornwall, to Aberdeen, Scotland. It was "daring" because the motorcar was fairly new to Britain, having only arrived there about 1895, the roads in most places were very poor, and the trip itself was 1,200 miles long.

As if the mere motor car ride itself was not demanding enough, William Booth planned to visit some 62 towns along the way and preach or lecture as often as four times a day. He would be, as some people described him, a kind of Toad (of The Wind in the Willows variety), racing around the countryside, perhaps landing in canals or being "pitched over a hedge." But General Booth had always been audacious and perhaps, in this venture some thought, just a little crazy.

The idea for a motorcar crusade came to him, he said, when he visited a small village that was difficult to reach by ordinary means. "The whole place appeared to come out to see me and bless me and touch me, and so I thought that if I could get about quickly from place to place—especially to those places not physically possible for one to reach by train—it would be a source of legitimate pleasure to the people and advantageous to the Kingdom. The motorcar suggested itself as the readiest method. Since then the idea has fermented, until now it has taken shape and form, and promises to be a success when carried out" [quoted in *Wiggins*, The History of The Salvation Army, Vol. V, p. 134].

FIVE-CAR FLEET

And a success it certainly was. With five automobiles in the 1904 fleet (some for the press and his traveling companions), the cavalcade was welcomed throughout rural Britain by "wildly cheering villagers," as well as by mayors, aldermen and church officials, who were often preached to by William Booth. It was something like a royal progress, writes Arch Wiggins, a bit of a show, but effective in making the Army better known [V: 133-45].

"This is one of the greatest, grandest, and one of the most effective efforts I have ever been privileged to make," wrote General Booth. "Some religious papers, they tell me, have been trying to belittle the effort by describing me as a showman. All right, I don't in the least object. I accept the application. For am I not flying through the land calling upon men and women to look at the accursed sins and vices that are eating out of their hearts the peace and purity and plenty God wants them to enjoy?"

SECOND TOUR

In the summer of 1905, just two days after William Booth arrived back from a tour of Australia and the Holy Land, he was off again on the second of his motor-tours, this time from Folkestone to Glasgow. The image of the well-known general, dressed in a dark-green motor coat and sitting (or sometimes standing when stopped) in a big white Darracq with red wheels, was commonly displayed in newspapers and magazines throughout Britain. As it would be again for every summer motor crusade (except 1910) until he died in 1912.

In between, he conducted business, convened international congresses, was received at Buckingham Palace by Edward VII, was created an Honorary Doctor of Laws at Oxford University, and was given the freedom of the cities of London and Nottingham. And he also traveled abroad: to the continent several times, to Australia and New Zealand in 1905, and finally in March-May 1907 a 25,000 mile trip to Japan (through Canada) and in September a return trip to the United States. Indefatigable? Obsessed? Whatever the epithet, his accomplishments were nothing short of amazing.

William Booth's first brief visit to New York in 1907 was nothing more than a stopover while he awaited his transportation to Canada on his way ultimately to Japan. It was to be strictly a "private appearance," made mainly, he said, to see his daughter, Eva, who had taken command of the United States in November 1904. She had done so to relieve her still-grieving brother-in-law, Frederick Booth-Tucker, whose wife, Emma, had so tragically died in October 1903.

A FAMILY'S TRAGEDY

That had been four years ago, but still the aging general thought daily of his "precious" Emma—lamenting her untimely death and praising her virtues. The poignant pictures of the much-loved "consul" gently guiding her elderly father to the platform, standing just behind him as he spoke to reporters, gently reminding him not to overtax himself and seeing him safely into his carriage were often recalled by him when he returned to tour the nation later in the year.

Emma's death had come as a terrible shock to William, coming as it did just a few months after his visit in 1903. In late October 1903, she had begun a tour of several American cities, opening a Rescue Home in Buffalo, and then spending a week at Fort Amity, Colorado, to discuss with Colonel Holland, the national colonization secretary, the future of the farm colony project. Leaving there on the 28th, in the company of Colonel Holland, she stopped briefly in Kansas City to visit the men's Industrial Home before traveling by train to Chicago where she was to meet her husband.

They departed at six o'clock that evening, and shortly after, they were passing Dean Lake, Missouri. She and the colonel were engaged in conversation in the tourist car, the train ran into an open switch, left the tracks and crashed into a steel water tower. The rear cars piled into and on top of one another, and both Emma and Colonel Holland were seriously injured. The colonel survived, but Emma, suffering from a fractured skull, died on the rescue train on the way to the hospital.

The pain of the moment—for all involved, but especially for Frederick, his seven children, for Eva and the general—was almost impossible to bear. His diary entries offer some glimpse, albeit only a superficial one, of the shock and sense of loss.

WHAT HAS BROUGHT YOU HERE?

"Afternoon. Quietly sitting in my room, and gathering my senses after a refreshing little sleep. Commissioner——was announced. 'What has brought you here?' was my first inquiry. On this his face straightened out, and holding a foreign cable in his hand announced that he had brought bad news. I seized the paper, and was staggered to find it contained the announcement that the consul and Colonel Holland had been seriously injured in a railway accident in the far West.

"I was dazed. I read it again and again. 'The extent of injuries not known' was one of the sentences with which it closed. This gave me some ground for hope. But, alas, my hopefulness only lasted a short season, for in a few minutes the chief entered and I guessed the worst. 'You have further intelligence?' I queried. He assented. 'Worse?' I said. 'Yes,' he replied with a face unutterably expressive of the distress that was in his heart. 'Killed,' I gasped. He bowed his head. My most agonizing fears were realized, my darling Emma for this world was no more" [*Begbie*, II: 282].

I SHALL GO ON . . .

Throughout his journal, and in his compassionate letters to Bramwell and Eva, this father gives to voice—as well as words will allow him— his grief, but always adds his determination to continue his mission: "*I shall go on.* Time will dull the anguish, if it does not altogether heal the wound. Perhaps nothing will do this; anyway nothing will take away the pain altogether until once more I *embrace her blessed form on the plains of light, in company with our darling Mamma"* [Ibid, p. 285].

It was his moment of consolation, therefore, to spend a few days with Eva, who now filled the void in his life, as she had done in the hearts of so many American Salvationists. She had become, as Emma had before her, the "darling" of the American public, feted by wealthy philanthropists and influential politicians. "Booth-Tucker was," writes Edward McKinley, "a difficult act to follow, but circumstances allowed the general to appoint the ideal choice: his fourth daughter, Eva. He could not have known [though he must have had an intuition] that he was bestowing upon the Salvation Army in the United States its most colorful, exciting, controversial, and certainly its most durable commander" [*Marching to Glory* (1995): 121].

Eva, though nothing less than an adoring daughter, presented quite a contrast to her sister. She was, by all accounts, less like her mother and more like her father: strong-willed, imperious, somewhat vain, but a brilliant speaker (excelling in dramatic style), a forceful leader, and a devoted evangelist with a gift for music and song-writing (which most Booth children had). "Nor did her abilities as publicist end on the platform: she was particularly adept at charming the rich and securing large contributions to the Army . . . Take her for what she was in fact and fancy, Eva Booth was a phenomenon of historic proportions" [*McKinley*, 122].

A PUBLIC AURA

By 1907, when her father again traveled to the states, she had become an American icon—beloved by Salvationists and the public alike. Though her strong stand as a prohibitionist alienated some Americans, her quick response to the San Francisco earthquake in 1906, her compassionate care for the needy, her stage performance all across America as "Evangeline Booth in Rags", lent her a public aura that lasted throughout her tenure as commander.

And now, for a few days in March 1907, she had her father to herself, except for some business with the Army's leaders, a portrait or two, and, alas, some sessions with the press. For, no matter how private he tried to be, beagle-nosed reporters found him out and no sooner had he disembarked than they came crowding round, some eager to seek his views on world affairs; others, probing to find the sensational tidbit.

"TAINTED" MONEY

They focused on his oft-stated claim that he would take money from anyone—and was especially anxious to tap the pocketbooks of America's tycoons such as Rockefeller and Carnegie. "I have never seen Carnegie," he replied, "nor approached him in any way, but I have thought that my methods would commend themselves to him. But he does not seem to think he can help those who are down, while he has greatly helped those who are up."

But wouldn't money taken from such sources be somehow "tainted?" they persisted, referring to a charge that had been made against General Booth sometime earlier. William Booth knew what they were referring to. "The Marquis of Queensberry," he told them, "who laid down the rules of the boxing ring, once gave me $500. (Boxing was notoriously related to gambling—Ed.)

"We prayed together. He had lost his wife and I mine. We wept together and were both comforted. 'Are you going to take that filthy money?' a lady asked me. 'Certainly I am,' I replied, and she denounced me right away. I would take anything and I would wash it in the tears of widows and orphans. I would lay it on the altar of benevolent effort for the good of the cause" [NY Times, March 6, 1907]. Those last lines were too good not to report, as they were in most American newspapers with sub-headlines proclaiming "Booth Will Take 'Tainted' Money." They would have to wait, however, until General Booth returned in the fall to see if the wealthy financiers—the Morgans, Carnegies and Rockefellers—would, this time around, be more receptive to his idea of a university of humanity than they had been in 1903.

At least, he told reporters, he would give it another try. He would need, he admitted, a large sum of money—as much as $5,000,000 (about half to bring it into existence and half to fund it as an endowment). "The university's aim," he told the reporters (as he had already told them four years earlier), "will be to teach people the best methods of dealing with the poor and crushed of every description. Others expend a great deal of money for the educational benefit of the well to do, teaching arts and sciences. We shall try to have a university in which the poor, the starving unemployed, and the drunkard may be studied and methods devised for helping them" [Ibid]. It was bold and ambitious, and a plan which Eva Booth would be laying before several influential people while her father toured Japan. When he came back he would do his best to lay it before all Americans as a viable public venture.

A 20-Minute Photograph

Before he left for Canada, however, William Booth was persuaded to have his photograph taken—a moment which has left us with one of the most intimate photographs ever taken. And it was the amateur photographer, Lieutenant-Colonel Edward Justus Parker, who did so, the story of how the portrait came to be taken being as fascinating as the photo itself:

"In 1907 the founder went to Japan via the United States [actually via Canada]. During a very brief stopover in New York I requested permission to make some photographic studies. My request was granted, but in the rush and with the restrictions which accompanied the grant, I felt rather inclined to back out. First, I would be allowed 20 minutes; second, because of his busy day the pictures must be taken while he was at work at a desk in a room with large windows on three sides. To get anything satisfactory with light blazing into the camera lens would, of course, be impossible.

"However, I accepted the assignment and hurriedly secured some pieces of dark green cloth about six feet square. With these in the hands of two assistants, shading out the conflicting light, we got some negatives, of which this favored likeness is one. (See photo before Visit 4). I had placed the general at a desk in the act of writing. Had he remained in that position the picture would have been a profile.

"How Can I Be Writing?"

"When all was ready and I was about to trip the shutter, this grand old beloved man turned his face toward me and exclaimed, 'How can I be writing when there is no ink in this pen?' In that exclamation there was a glimpse into his character. I was not interested in his writing. That part of my instruction was a fake; to him it was real. I had told him to do what he could not do with an empty pen. Look at that portrait and study the expression on that noble face as he reprimands me with his, 'How can I be writing without ink?' By the image of photography that expression is preserved for all time. He could not relax to pose. Do you know that I am really glad there was no ink in that pen? A posed picture would not have been a true portrait" [*My Fifty-Eight Years*, pp. 232-33].

MEETING THE EMPEROR

After just three days, spent in private consultations and fireside relaxation, William Booth was off to Canada on his way to Japan. The month spent in the Far East, he later stated, afforded him the most stirring experiences of his career. Though the Salvation Army had not, and would never, make much headway in that country, its founder was accorded a gracious welcome. Twenty-five thousand people met him in Tokyo where he was received at the Imperial Palace by the emperor, and another 35,000 shouted a "banzai" at the railway station in Sendai.

It surpassed "everything in my whole life's history," General Booth wrote later, expressing a vain hope that Japan would become another Salvation Army stronghold. With great prescience, he added: "It is only a question of time when [Japan's] industries will be tutored with the most expert direction, and packed with the finest machinery taken from all nations of the world, and I do not see what can prevent her from producing the finest articles at the cheapest possible prices." He did not know, of course, the awful tragedies of war that Japan and the rest of the world would have to endure before that would happen.

Chapter Twenty-Five

When William Booth returned to America in September 1907, for what he called his "final farewell" tour, he was no longer just "General" or "Reverend," but was entitled to be called "Doctor." The honorary degree, doctor of civil law, had been conferred on him in June by Oxford University, yet another acknowledgment that the world had accepted him as one of its great social benefactors. "This is probably one of the few honors which you would be willing to accept," wrote Lord Curzon in his invitation.

"To me it would be an even higher honor to be the instrument of conferring it, for I should like the famous and ancient university, of which I am now the head, and which has played so notable a part in the history of our country—to have the privilege of setting its seal upon the noble work that you have done for so many years, and are continuing to do, for the people of all countries—a work excelled in range and benef-icence by that of no living man" [*Begbie* II: 355]. In the company of such great men as Mark Twain, Sir Evelyn Wood, Auguste Rodin, Rudyard Kipling and Camille Saint-Saëns, William Booth donned the robe of academe partly as a personal honor but also, by acceptance, to promote still further the work of the Salvation Army.

But it was a title he carried lightly, rarely flaunting it before the public, remaining as always a preacher of the simple gospel of salvation. And the bold headlines which described his efforts: "Salvation for the World," "General Booth, at 79, Still Works to Evangelize the World," and "General Booth Wins 194 Converts" captured the essence of his mission. His "final farewell" would be, to his soldiers and the American public, a cry for unceasing war against the unremitting evils of sin and poverty. "The Salvation Army is not a creed," he told them; "it is a movement. It is a continuous revival, all the year round. It is more than a raid in the darkness of night and a race back (which is easy in war). That is differ-ent from capturing a country and conquering a city. That is what the

Salvation Army is doing, and there is more yet to do" [*Boston Globe,*
Sept. 30].

DELVING DOWN

"The Salvation Army," he promised, " is going to continue to go 'down.'
By this I mean that we are to continue to minister to those who are sunk
in sin and wickedness. The danger which confronts nearly all religions
and theologies is the danger to rise, to rise above the level of the men
and women who have made them and whom they have made.

"We must delve down, down. Our mission, our work, is among the
neglected class—the people who pay the $5 and $20 fines. Therefore,
we must continue to go lower, to keep down, and not rise above the
heads of those we seek to save. Our endeavor must be among those who
are beyond the pale of the ordinary effort.

"Let the theologians and the philosophers have their sacramental
doings. With these things the Salvation Army has nothing to do. We have
to stick to that half-damned crowd; we must lift them up and give them
a chance at the better things. So long as the Army sticks to that, so long
will it prosper; when it departs from this path, it is not desirable that it
should live longer. There are plenty of other people to do the ceremoni-
als" [*Washington Times,* Oct. 28, 1907].

LOOKING FORWARD

One other theme he pursued, another promise he gave. When asked
about the future of the Army, most specifically what would happen to it
when he died, he replied: "Well, thank God, the general is not dead yet,
and hasn't made up his mind to die, but rather to live as long as he possibly can. But if the angel of death should come and call me away, here
in this ancient city of Boston today, the same news flashed over the electric wires all over the world would be accompanied by a shout, 'Long
live the general!' Arrangements have already been made that when one
general steps off the stage, another will step on" [*Globe,* Sept. 30].

That William Booth seemed unlikely to die soon was the general
consensus of the press. He was, as they soon discovered, still lively,
witty and opinionated. "Those Americans who will hear and see General

Booth during the eight weeks' inspection of the Salvation Army in this country," wrote one, "will find that age has marked the noteworthy man lightly, while time has not in the least lessened his enthusiasm for the contest which he began 43 years ago against sin and misery.

"At the age of 79 [actually 78] the venerable head of the Salvation Army has but one infirmity, a slight affection of the hearing. He sleeps lightly, but there is no indication of age in the bright eye which glistens beneath the heavy eyebrows, and the clear, strong voice. The whitened, tangled hair and the beard speak of advanced years, but there seems to be an abundant vitality for years of further work in his chosen field" [*Fitchburgh Daily Sentinel*, Sept. 30]. The report from the *Rochester Democrat and Chronicle* where General Booth visited on October 3, adds further to the impression of vitality and offers a description typical of most:

"While drums rolled and trumpets proclaimed the advance of the marching legion of the Salvation Army, in front of Central Church last night, a crowd that couldn't hope to pass into the overcrowded edifice stood in the rain and pushed and jostled one another in an effort to get a glimpse of the head of the Salvation Army, an army that has been built from nothing by a man whose far-famed piety and power has thrown the circle of its influence around the world.

A Sense of Humor

"The man they saw, General William Booth, looked the part—a patriarchal sort of man, tall, with flowing silvery beard and straggling silvery hair; buttoned up tightly in a plain black-braided coat that had but the hint of uniform to it; a thin, ascetic face whose radiant smile seemed to reflect something of the beauty of the life that he has given to the service of those whom he calls his brothers and sisters. His eyes, clear and bright, for all of his age, are full and expressive, with an occasional promise of humorous appreciation which is amply fulfilled when he speaks on the platform. Like all great men, General Booth has the saving sense—the sense of humor.

"When he speaks his words come with a rush, as if from an overfull heart. His enunciation is well nigh perfect, and his tones are as clear and ringing as those of many an orator half his age. It seemed that everyone in all of the great audience must have caught every tone inflection, every syllable of his address. There is no sign of age diminishing his intellectual powers or eloquence. He spoke very simply, words, manner, and attitude carrying the perfect conviction of perfect faith. While supposedly speaking from the subject "The Past, Present, and Future of the Salvation Army," he wandered delightfully from his speech at times, interlacing his speech with all sorts of anecdotes and incidents—pathetic, humorous, and illuminating. At intervals he preached with solemn earnestness the doctrine of the atonement, which is the only theology the Salvation Army knows" [Oct. 4].

SOCIAL VIEWS

But as much as William Booth loved to preach, and was single-minded in his promotion of universal salvation, he was not averse to giving opinions on all sorts of current social practices. At his press conferences he dispensed them freely and vigorously. He was, he said, in favor of large families, believing that small ones fostered indulgence, which bred recklessness among the children. Large families, he maintained, were a blessing, and it was better to have many children to care for you in old age than to rely on a system of old-age pensions which simply promoted idleness in old age.

As for divorce, though he did not agree with it in principle, and felt that American divorce laws were too encouraging of the practice, he nevertheless thought there were instances where divorce was necessary and the best remedy to impossible marriages. "In some families where divorces have been granted, I have found cases where I should not want to take either side. I can only imagine what I should have done had I been placed as those people were."

ROLE OF WOMEN

The question was related, in some way, to the role of women in society. While William Booth felt that the "divine plan" was one which designated the female as family care-giver, he was certain that women could play a useful role in society (as his female officers were demonstrating), and, perhaps, some of the problems then being experienced by women in America (such as extreme boredom, social drinking, etc.) were the result of a lack of fulfillment as a human being. "I cannot refrain from speaking," declared General Booth, "on the terrible fact that drunkenness and other vices are on the increase among women, not in their old forms, but equally degrading, demoralizing and damaging.

"Perhaps the chief cause is the absence in our educational and religious system of the insistence upon a definite and useful purpose in life. Hence many women seek in recreation and 'tonics' the intangible something which they can only find in a noble life work. They convert innocent games into gambling, abuse social pleasures and form unwomanly habits. Look at the women of the Salvation Army. They are the happiest in the world because they live for a purpose" [*Des Moines Daily News*, Oct. 12].

ON APATHY AND WEALTH

When asked about the growing apathy towards religion, he replied: "the indifference to religion is growing because so many have tried it and not found the satisfaction that they have expected, so they have turned from it." He did not think there was any prejudice against religion, just that the increasing force with which worldly attractions were brought before the people had something to do with public disinterest. And when asked if he thought a rich man would enter heaven, he replied with a laugh that it depended on what he did with his money. If he gave it to the Salvation Army, he [the general] would be pleased to say a word or two to St. Peter at the gate on behalf of the rich man.

Still in a philosophic mood, William Booth gave his personal recipe for fulfillment. "Some men find their life's pleasure in painting a fine picture, in composing a song, in dissecting the human form. I find mine in remolding a man's soul. Believe me, it is interesting work. The cause of the suffering in this world is mostly selfishness. Everyone is selfish. Even children are selfish. Give them two apples and they want three. Everyone should try to eliminate this from their nature, to work together, not for possession but for the good of one another." And to the *Des Moines Daily News* he gave what he called his life's "credo."

WILLIAM BOOTH'S TENETS

"My work is my pleasure, my amusement. It has been 16 years since I had a holiday. I work seven days a week and as many hours each day as I can keep going."

"What I do, I do for the love of it. I don't ride in a motorcar; I don't live in a swell mansion; I don't eat out of a gold bowl with a silver spoon, but I do practice what I preach.

"Here's my religion: Love God with all your heart and your neighbor as yourself. Try to make others good by being good yourself.

"Let your moderation be known to all men.

"Prayer is useless unless a person's life and actions harmonize with it.

"If I ask God to do my work for me, he will decline with thanks.

"The divine work in this world is through human agency, unity, cooperation.

"I never expect to retire from my work until I get orders from above.

"I have been asked what I intend to do. Most assuredly not run a newspaper or go into politics.

"I would like to be a citizen of this country. I would like to be a citizen of Japan and Russia and France, and in every country where I could lay the foundation of universal citizenship.

"I love America and Americans. They have been most kind and generous in their support of my work.

"I try to save the souls of the people. Even newspapermen can be saved."

The newspaper reporters loved that last maxim, and made sure it was included as a final punch line. For William Booth was still a reporter's ideal interviewee, very quick with an appropriate rejoinder to every smart query or quip. When, for example, someone suggested to him, in a paraphrase of Robert Burns' words, "Man's inhumanity to man makes a whole world mourn," he quickly demonstrated his ready optimism by countering: 'Yes, but man's humanity to man makes a whole world happy, too.'"
That, it seems, neatly summed up his whole philosophy.

Chapter Twenty-Six

For most of the 1907 tour William Booth was, as one reporter commented, "a bundle of energy, a keg of dynamite, an example of perpetual motion." In spite of his 78 years, he exuded vitality. He demonstrated as much even before he reached America by giving a two-hour lecture on the Army aboard the *Virginian* as he sailed from Liverpool to Rimouski, Quebec. One of his fellow travelers was Signor Marconi, the famous inventor of wireless telegraphy, and it was he who chaired William Booth's shipboard lecture. He had, he stated in his introduction, been an admirer of the Army since a boy of seven. When Senator Gibson publicly thanked General Booth for his inspiring talk, he humorously imagined him in the new Jerusalem communicating with Marconi and sending back descriptions of heaven by wireless telegraphy.

He was, his shipboard listeners thought, at the peak of his powers. And on all fronts, from his first meetings in Boston (September 27) to his meetings in St. Louis on October 12-13, he certainly seemed to be so. His receptions were magnanimous and his speeches and sermons extolled. Though the newspaper coverage was perhaps less extensive than in previous years, and often appeared on the third or fourth pages as opposed to the first, it was no less enthusiastic. For, while the Fourth Estate might now be less interested in William Booth's non-American social ventures, they were nevertheless still very positive about the Army's contribution to American religious life and society.

As an example of the celebrity status which he now enjoyed, we might look at his reception in the city of Des Moines, Iowa, which he visited on October 15. Even before he arrived, the *Des Moines Daily News* was preparing its readers for the special treat that was to be theirs.

GRAND OLD MAN

"Pushing speedily westward from the far eastern states is a gaunt framed, snowy-haired, eagle-eyed old man. He is due to arrive in Des Moines on October 15.

"And there is feverish activity in the ranks of the local Salvation Army. Just as Uncle Sam's Army polishes its rifles till they shine like silver when a great general is coming on a tour of inspection, so is the Salvation Army preparing for the visit of this gaunt-framed, white-haired old man.

"For he is none other than General Booth, head and founder of the Salvation Army of the world. Once a restless sapling of a youth with the fire of a great mission burning in his heart, he is now an old man who has accomplished that mission and commands thousands of its workers all over the world. The Salvation Army reveres and loves Miss Eva Booth. But it looks almost with awe upon the grand old man who is its chief.

"Those who have seen the general are proudly telling the less fortunate ones what he looks like, his personal characteristics and little anecdotes concerning him. Those who have not seen him are looking forward to his visit to Des Moines as one of the greatest pleasures of their lives.

HOVEL AND PALACE

"Note the way in which a Salvation Army man speaks the name of General Booth. There is invariably a reverent lowering of the voice, an inflection of great pride. Had it not been for this 78-year old man, it is very likely there would be no singing groups of Salvation Army lassies on the streets today. There would be no such ready hand stretched forth to help the poor and friendless.

"And not only the Salvationists, but the whole city is looking forward with interest to the coming of General Booth. It is not every day we meet a man who has preached salvation to fashionable audiences and to lepers, convicts, emigrants and homeless outcasts. The hovel and the palace have figured alike in his remarkable career. He has been honored by presidents, kings, emperors, governors, senators, nobles and public men of all creeds and opinions. Perhaps the most remarkable of these many receptions was the one tendered by the mikado of Japan. The ovation he received in Japan has few if any equals in the history of that country.

"The zeal which characterized General Booth as a youth has never left him. Those who know him well say it is his devout and fervent submission to God which leaves the greatest impression on his followers. While they may differ with him in opinion, they never doubt his honesty and disinterestedness of motive" (Oct. 15).

DIETARY SPECIFICS

Like every city on this visit, Des Moines went out of its way to ensure that the general's every need should be met. Especially was it important to pay attention to his gastronomic needs:

"General William Booth of the Salvation Army will find his three meals prepared by the Savery chef exactly as he has ordered them by telegraph. Not only that, the general sends on the recipe for the vegetable soup which is his chief article of diet . . . However lavishly the general is entertained or however daintily prepared a dinner is in Des Moines, he will not deviate one iota from his accustomed menu. He is a strict vegetarian and eats sparingly of butter or grease. At midnight he eats another meal, a duplicate in form of the breakfast and supper.

"For dinner the general has ordered vegetable soup, baked potato and no butter. This is his recipe for the soup: one carrot, one turnip, one small onion, chopped parsley, one teaspoon pearl barley and a piece of butter the size of a walnut. The other meals will be tea, boiled milk and toast with no butter. He will have none of any flesh, fish or fowl" [Semi-Weekly *Waterloo Courier*, Oct. 8].

TALKS THAT THRILLED

As in Des Moines, so in his subsequent meetings in Minneapolis and Milwaukee, William Booth thrilled his audiences with his lecture on "The Secret of the Success of The Salvation Army." He spoke of the worldwide movement; the discouragements and the encouragements; the thousands of homes made happy; the many wanderers reclaimed, and he illustrated them with personal anecdotes and poignant stories. On all

such occasions the auditorium was filled with "well-known people representing the official, the religious, the educational and the social life"
of the cities. The staff band from Chicago enlivened the programs and
"cheers and waving handkerchiefs also greeted Miss Eva Booth when
her venerable father introduced her to the audience, putting his arms
about her and kissing her fondly as he said, 'This is my daughter.'"
Everyone applauded, and went home feeling confident of the in-
domitability of the Army's venerable leader.

ILLNESS STRIKES

On the morning of October 18, however, reports flashed across America
and, by cable, to England, that William Booth was critically ill—some re-
leases stating he was near death. It was the first time in many years that
he was forced to seek medical assistance, take a week to recover, and,
most serious to his pride, cancel an engagement. But the mere fact that
he did, and that he returned to Chicago for medical treatment, was indication enough of a serious illness. In his diary entry for October 19, his
secretary, Fred Cox, made this statement: "Late Saturday morning. A lot
of things have happened. I have sat up, or rather stood up, all night with
the general. We had a consultation of two of the leading doctors here
last night, and they say the g. has catarrh of the appendix, which may
lead to appendicitis."

IN GOOD HANDS

Even then, Cox could not refrain from a little levity. "We have with us,"
he wrote, "an S.A. nurse; she has a nose like a stiletto, and motions like
lightning. She is very short and very fiery. When she came up into the
room she swooped down like an eagle on its prey. 'Now, Mr. Booth,' she
chirped in her best American, 'I want to feel your pulse.' She seized his
wrist like a vice and jammed the clinical thermometer halfway down his
throat, laid her hand on his brow and then snorted, 'There, Mr. Booth,
I've fixed you up all right, I guess.' Then she snapped out of the room
like a catherine-wheel off its pin."

But the episode, in spite of Cox's usual lightheartedness, was very
serious. Feverish, and often delirious, the general was nursed through
his illness by his daughter, Eva, and by Cox and, after a week's rest and

treatment, was given permission to resume his tour. This he did on October 25, in Columbus, Ohio (having missed a four-day engagement in Cleveland), continuing on through Pittsburgh, Washington, Baltimore, Philadelphia and New York. And he did so in what most observers called "an exhausted state," often attended by local doctors to see that he did not relapse.

On the train from Columbus to Pittsburgh, for example, he again collapsed and two physicians were asked by telegraph to meet him at the station. "The aged man," reported the *New York Times*, "had to be assisted to a carriage; he was hurried to the hotel where the physicians took him in hand." He was suffering from no particular ailment, they said, but had simply been overcome by overwork.

FORTITUDE

And yet, the aging general would not give in! On the day following his five-day illness he gave one sermon and two lectures! "All last night," reported the *New York Times*, "he was so ill that two physicians were with him constantly, and they accompanied him to the theater this morning. Although feeble, he talked for *an hour and 20 minutes* at the meeting this afternoon on the work of the Salvation Army. At the morning and evening services he delivered sermons" [Oct 27].

And, though he showed signs of lingering frailty, he continued a hectic round of public and private engagements. In Washington D.C. (on the 28th) he again dined with President Roosevelt who had now become a close friend and gave his opinion that "there is no more effective method of evangelizing a people than with a brass band. I confess I like brass bands, and I like your brass bands." Describing this occasion in his journal, Booth wrote:

WHITE HOUSE LUNCHEON

"The last time I lunched at the White House I met nearly all the members of the Cabinet and there were no ladies, but on this occasion I suppose they thought the presence of Eva—one lady—demanded the presence of others also. Whether their company made the interview more profitable or not, it certainly did not render it any less agreeable.

"On entering we were welcomed by an attendant who took charge of our wraps, then we shook hands with a couple of other gentlemen of whom we had no knowledge, and then, conducted by a youthful looking Cavalry officer—a Captain Ney by name—into an inner room, we found Commissioner McFarland and his lady with Mrs. Cortelyou. We had a nice little talk; all seemed deeply interested in what we were doing, and the commissioner, who they say is the most influential man in Washington local affairs, repeated over and over again that he would be delighted to do anything he could to assist us. This gentleman will preside at my meeting tonight.

"At this point, accompanied by Captain Ney, the president came in with a nice little friendly bounce, and shook hands all round, and then commenced a conversation, but had not proceeded far before Mrs. Roosevelt, dressed up in what I suppose would be considered a luxurious and gorgeous fashion, entered the apartment.

"I had not met her before; she did the lady of the house in a very cheerful manner, and we formed up, the president and his lady leading the way.

"Eva sat on the president's right hand at one table, and I was honored with a similar place by Mrs. Roosevelt at the opposite end, Mrs. McFarland sitting to my right, and she and I were soon engaged in conversation.

ROOSEVELT'S CURIOSITY

"A great deal was said and a good many questions were asked that showed that the president was interested in the Salvation Army. Amongst other things he expressed his curiosity as to the way the Army in one nationality dealt with that of another in the way of government. He did not see how the American could deal with the English, and the German with the Scot, and so on, and so on. On this subject we gave him information in which Eva, being the nearest to him, took the lion's share.

"The president expressed his admiration that we raised officers of each nationality, and said the fact gave him real pleasure.

"Commissioner McFarland interposed the remark, 'Interesting as the subject is, I am sure the president would be pleased to hear about the Oxford function; would the general sketch it out? All about Lord

Curzon, and so on' [refers to the general's award of an honorary Oxford doctorate that year—Ed.].

"The president at once said, 'Yes, General, I would like to hear about it very much.' Whereupon I described the scene, in all of which details he appeared much interested.

"Then came another suggestion from McFarland, saying that some facts concerning my recent visit to Japan would surely be of interest to the president. This gave me the opportunity of describing my visit and also giving my own convictions with regard to that country, specially dwelling upon the quiet manner in which the nation took their recent triumph in the late war [the Sino-Japanese war (1894-95) which marked the emergence of Japan as a major world power].

CHINA AND JAPAN

"I ventured to make the suggestion that this was the opportunity for the nation dealing with Japan to cultivate friendliness, specially in view of the possible coming power and activity of China; to which the president made a very natural reply for a man of his position, that he thought it would pay to cultivate friendliness with China, and then the conversation wandered away again to the future of the Army, and so on, until the hour had passed and the signal was given for adjournment.

"We rose to our feet, the president took my hand in his, and assured me of the pleasure the visit had given him, and with a general handshake we parted.

"There was not as much dignity, seriousness, and intelligence about this visit as I should have liked, or indeed expected, still it served the Army to good purpose and will do still more in the days to come" [*Begbie*, II: 355-56].

Chapter Twenty-Seven

In Philadelphia (on October 31) the general was presented with the Freedom of the City, an electric key being suspended from the arch of City Hall, an honor which, according to the *Philadelphia Ledger*, no military hero had ever received. And in New York, though he "showed plainly the effects of the severe illness which he suffered in the West," he conducted what he called a "whirlwind campaign for souls." He met the press on Friday, spoke at three meetings in the Amsterdam Theater on Sunday (Nov. 3), gave a public lecture at Carnegie Hall on Monday (his formal welcome to the city), addressed three councils of his American officers, attended to a great deal of Army business with his daughter Eva, and made his farewell speech on Friday, November 8, before sailing back to Europe on the *St. Louis* the following day.

The three Sunday meetings were the emotional highlights of the week. "At each meeting," stated the *New York Times*, "the orchestra and balconies were crowded and demonstrations of the wildest enthusiasm were made in response to the exhortations of the aged evangelist. In the course of the three meetings 194 persons left their seats in the theater and went up on the stage in public acknowledgment of their conversion. Nearly 300 uniformed workers in the Salvation Army sat on the stage behind the general, the red markings on the uniforms of the men, the red ribbons on the bonnets of the women, and the red vests which several of the officers wore flecking with color the otherwise soberly garbed crowd . . .

"Throughout the general's addresses there was a constant undertone of murmured approbation from the members of the Salvation Army and the audience, rising at times to the proportions of a chanting accompaniment. General Booth referred several times to his present illness and to his regret that his present weakness made it impossible for him to conduct the whole service, as he used to do" [Oct. 4].

PROFESSION WITHOUT POSSESSION

In his sermons William Booth dwelt on the need to experience "real" religion and to do away with what he called "unsatisfactory, unsatisfying, and hollow sham. Blessed, indeed," he said, "are they who hunger and thirst after righteousness, but blessed also are they who attain it. There are some people who never get beyond the religion of resolution, the often-expressed desire to do something good and self-sacrificing which never becomes anything more real than a desire. In religion, profession without possession means the utmost misery. And the possession of a real religion means the readiness to work for the salvation of others. What salvation can a man have in his religion when his wife or his children or his friends are going astray before his very eyes? What comfort to a man can the image of the dying Christ be unless he himself is dying to sin? Oh, with what gladness I recall the joy I felt when 63 years ago I came for the first time to the mercy seat and resolved to carry the great message to my fellow-man."

ALTAR CALL

At the end of his sermon came his passionate plea: "O, the beauty of goodness! O, the beauty of truth! O, the beauty of purity! O, the beauty of love! Don't you want to know what they are, to feel them, to live for them, die with them? Don't you want your last hour on this earth to be sweet—a triumphal exit from this world, a triumphal entry into the next? Change ye, change ye. In the twinkling of an eye, then, it will be as hard for you to do wrong as it is now for you to do right. Come and be emancipated. Come and belong to the free people of the Lord. All for Jesus. Won't you come to the river of life and bathe in its pellucid waters?"

After his sermons were over, General Booth left the theater to rest. "The meeting was after that conducted by Colonel John Lawley, who led most of the hymns and who sang some solos, and by Colonel Gifford. One hundred and three converts mounted the stage at the last meeting. When the hundredth had come into view Colonel Gifford clapped his hands with delight and, at a suggestion from Colonel Nichol, led the officers in procession around the stage, singing hymns as they went" [NY Times, Oct. 4].

LONG LIVE THE GENERAL

At his public lecture in Carnegie Hall, attended by the elite of New York, William Booth gave what he termed his "farewell greeting" to America, hastening to add that this should not be construed as a sign of failing health. "It has been asked," he said, "what is to become of the Salvation Army when the general passes away. I say, don't worry, the general is not dead yet." Here he was interrupted by applause and shouts of well wishes that continued for many minutes. When he could make himself heard again, he continued: "The general has found his life to be so valuably regarded by those about him that he will live as long as possible. Yet I am conscious in the hours that I feel the vital juices flowing (and I am rapidly beginning to feel better after my recent illness), that even if the death angel were to come to me before midnight arrangements have been made, so far as is possible to make them with the best legal aid and supplications to God, so that another general would step upon the stage. To the message, 'The general is dead,' could be added, 'Long live the general.'"

INTRODUCING NEW TECHNOLOGY

General Booth's "final farewell" to his soldiers and the people of America was staged in the open air on Friday evening, November 8. Some 5,000 people awaited his message. The Salvationists themselves had marched from the Army's headquarters on Fourteenth Street with "torches blazing, bands playing, and the big banner held aloft, 'General Booth Says Good-Bye to New York, City Hall, Tonight.'" Acting as magnets, the Salvationists were followed by "as picturesque an array as ever followed a procession in this city" [*NY Times*, Nov. 9]. An innovative feature of the event was a succession of scenes of the Salvation Army's work, intermingled with Scripture quotes, flashed on a giant screen strung between the pillars of the hall, projected there by a relatively new invention, a stereopticon. Most people had never witnessed anything like it.

When General Booth arrived in an automobile, at 15 minutes past nine, accompanied by his daughter, Eva, "a path was opened for him through the crowd, and he ascended to the topmost step, then turned and faced the enormous crowd, the light from the stereopticon full upon him. For an instant he stood here in silence, and then the crowd set up such a cheering that the people came running to the windows of the sky-scrapers near by. Then when the cheering ceased the general uncovered his gray locks and began his speech, which in itself was something re-markable" [Ibid]. To the people assembled he said, slowly so that his words could be repeated to the large crowd by three strategically placed Army officers with megaphones:

SALVATION FOR ALL

"Comrades and friends: We have had a mighty time together. I leave you with confidence in your love; with confidence in your loyalty; confi-dence in your perseverance; confidence that the war will go on.

"Be true to your principles. Be true to your Master. Stand by His cross as He stood by you. Be true to your commander. She has the love of my soul. Keep up the fight for God. Keep up the fight for the salvation of souls, the true greatness of the nation. Uplift the downtrodden. Make men and women savers of each other's souls.

"Salvation for everybody! [Cheers] Salvation for the president! [Cheers]. Salvation for the government! Salvation for the people! Salva-tion for the police! [Laughter] Salvation for the United States! Salvation for poor old England! [Laughter] Salvation for the world!

"Win America for Jesus. Fight while you live. Meet me in heaven. You have nearly killed me with kindness. But I am going to recuperate on the steamer. Glory to God in the highest! . . . Good-bye till we meet again. I'll come and see you when I'm dead, if they'll let me. Glory to God. Ten thousand hallelujahs. Amen. Amen. Fire a volley! ['Amen!' 'Amen!' 'Amen!']

"Here Commander Eva Booth interjected, 'Careful, father—you're killing yourself,' whereupon the general concluded his epigrammatic ad-dress by the words, 'God be with you till we meet again.'"

"Meanwhile," concluded the *New York Times* reporter, "the photog-raphers had been busy all around, and the constant pop of flashlights punctuated the general's speech. At its close, the word was given and the stereopticon flashed on the screen behind the general the words of the hymn, 'God Be With You Till We Meet Again.' The Salvationists started singing the hymn, and everybody there joined in the singing, un-til the motormen stopped their cars on Broadway to listen, and the clerks came pouring out of the back door of the post office.

"After the first verse had been sung General Booth whispered to the men with the megaphones. 'Let everyone who is a Christian lift up his right hand as he sings the second verse.' The word went forth and the Salvationists obeyed instantly and started singing again. Of those on the outskirts of the crowd, a few hung back, but soon their hands went up, too. After the hymn was finished the crowd gave three rousing cheers for General Booth. Then a passageway was made through the crowd for him again, and he re-entered his automobile and was driven away."

FINAL GOODBYE

After the farewell ceremony, General Booth gave the press a dictated message for the American people:

"Farewell America: you have given me a right generous welcome. On this visit I have seemed to come nearer to the heart of the nation than on any other occasion. Fain would I have stayed longer with you. Indeed, I would have wished that some method might have been invented by which I could have been constituted one of your own sons and so taken a practical step towards the realization of that fatherhood of the people which must of necessity be the first step to that brotherhood of nations on which so many hearts are set. But I understand this to be impossible without sacrificing my fatherland. Nothing can prevent, however, my living in the spirit of that relationship, and in that spirit I shall think of you and pray for you as I go forward on the path towards which the beckoning finger of duty invites.

"My visit here has been a busy, and I hope a useful one. It has served, among other things, to reveal to me the fact of the improved understanding as to the objects and methods of the Army, together with the existence of a higher appreciation of its value and influence. Many of your leaders in thought, commerce, politics and religion have said so in a most emphatic manner at the great gatherings which I have been privileged to hold.

HIGHEST HAPPINESS

"The press, which, if anywhere under the sun, is here a true exponent of the mind of the nation, has also said so in unmistakable terms. In fact, your confidence and sympathy have made me hope for your hearty

co-operation in carrying out the great program to which I have consecrated my life. That program contains the highest happiness and the
truest welfare in this world and the world to come, not only of every citizen, high or low, but of every member of the human race.

"With every assurance of my prayers and toils in all that concerns
the honor and righteousness of your flag and confident of the future triumph of the principles on which the Army is founded, I remain, yours in
the bond of faithful friendship, William Booth."

"While he promises to return if he lives," wrote one reporter, "the
Salvationists who heard him say good-bye last night seemed to feel that
they would not see him again, this side of the great divide." For most
Americans (except the few who were lucky enough to travel to England), that estimate proved true. General Booth did not again set foot
on American soil. But he did impress his personality on both the Salvation Army in America and on the nation itself.

Chapter Twenty-Eight

Assessing William Booth's final visit to the United States is a difficult task. As a "final farewell" to his troops, and to those many Americans who had come to love him, it was an unmitigated success. General Booth had been the ideal visitor, accessible, charming, and delightfully outspoken. Most Salvationists were also thrilled by his presence, for he obviously toughened their spiritual resolve.

CLEARLY A TWO-FOLD MISSION

Lillian Taiz, in her excellent book, *Hallelujah Lads and Lasses* (2001), wrote: "During the early twentieth century the Salvation Army ceased to be a working-class-dominated religious organization devoted to advertising salvation to others like themselves with lively and boisterous expressions of spirituality. Instead, the organization served an increasingly segmented constituency; its social institutions offered temporal salvation to the poor while its spiritual work ministered to upwardly mobile second and third generations of previously working-class Salvationist families. In contrast to the blood-washed warriors of the nineteenth century, Salvationists in the twentieth century gradually regarded themselves as members of a church that sponsored professionalized Christian social services to the downtrodden" [p. 144].

William Booth continued to see the Army as he had done some 30 years before, believing that Salvationists would continue to be the nonconformists of the religious world; that the Army would be a mighty evangelical force in America; and that the social and evangelical wings would remain an integrated mission.

HOLDING ON TO DREAMS

William Booth was, by nature, an inveterate idealist, always a visionary, and always a fighter. Among his last words were those now quoted so often: "While women weep, as they do now, I'll fight; while little children grow hungry, as they do now, I'll fight; while men go to prison, in and out, in and out, as they do now, I'll fight; while there is a drunkard left, while there is a poor lost girl upon the streets, while there remains one dark soul without the light of God, I'll fight—I'll fight to the very end!"

Though William Booth would never say "Never!" and therefore did not rule out the possibility of another visit to the United States, this was to be his final campaign in a country and among a people he had grown to love. Within two years, his eyesight was failing badly and, within four years his health had deteriorated nearly to the point of extreme fragility. He died on August 20, 1912, shortly after the sinking of the Titanic.

ONE OF THE GREATS

Americans, as did people around the world, mourned his death and wrote tributes to his life he would have been pleased to see. But, before he died he knew the heart-felt affection of Americans and lived to read tributes as effusive as any that would be written after he had "laid down his sword." He would, for example, read this one written by the journalist Robertus Love and, though we don't know what he thought of it, we suspect he was very proud to have been so highly regarded:

"Who is the greatest general in the history of the world?

"Several millions of men and women throughout the world, if asked that question, would reply instantly:

'General William Booth, Founder and Commander in Chief of the Salvation Army.'

"Most of these millions of enthusiasts no doubt are soldiers duly enlisted and enrolled in General Booth's Army. But there are many outsiders—earnest, studious, observing, intelligent and intellectual men and women—who would make the same reply to the question. They believe that General Booth is the most useful man on earth.

"The time has passed when newspapers put quotation marks around the military title of William Booth. This title, this rank, was of course not conferred by any nation and is not governmentally official. Nor did the Reverend Mr. Booth assume it himself. It was conferred upon him by his Army, and he has justified it by his work. He is a full general. The army he commands is greater by far than any that was commanded by Alexander or Hannibal or Napoleon or Grant. It is the biggest army that ever happened, and its battlefront and firing line are longer than all the battlefronts and firing lines of the past put together. The line reaches around the world, penetrates and crisscrosses 49 nations and has hopes of reaching into Russia, the fiftieth.

SOAP, SOUP AND SALVATION

"His is the Salvation Army—its mission is to save rather than slay. It slays a devil wherever one's head pops up, but it saves men and women—millions of them; saves them not only spiritually, according to the orthodox creeds of Christendom, but saves them physically; saves them from themselves and from society, which has negatively neglected them or positively ground them underfoot.

"General Booth is a great muckraker. He has taken his rake and gone down into the muck of the 'submerged tenth,' the outcast, the criminal, the pauperized, the despairing, the helpless and hopeless people of God's world, and he has raked them up into the light of day, given them soap to wash off the muck, given them soup to feed their starving stomachs and then talked spiritual salvation to them. Judging from what we know of the character and teachings of Christ, the Man of Galilee would do pretty much likewise if on earth today" [*Newark Daily Advocate*, March 19, 1907].

Such unstinted praise, reiterated across the nation, must have affirmed William Booth's belief that his visits to America had been eminently worthwhile. By his efforts—though not his alone, he would have said—the Salvation Army had, by 1907, reached a pinnacle of public popularity from which it has never fallen.

Appendix A

"What Was the Inner History of the Origin of the Salvation Army?" General William Booth's Answer at the Boston Lecture at Park Street Church, Monday Noon, February18th, 1895

Stenographically reported by Mr. J.C. Miller, and purposely left without revision.

Dr. Cook, Ladies and Gentlemen: I feel altogether unequal, I am sure, in my own estimation, to the task of speaking to this audience in anything like an interesting and profitable manner. I have just come from a very trying meeting in Faneuil Hall, and I have two other large meetings before me today; and I am a little wearied, not only in body, but in mind, with the exercises of yesterday. And I have no particular topic before me, except the topic on which I am always talking, until I have almost, I think, talked myself out, and talked everybody else's patience out upon that topic. And that is the Salvation Army. And I have this consolation, that I have no doubt it is on that question that you would like to hear me say something. (Applause.) Some ministers were dragging me into a ministerial meeting against my will, against my protest, the other day, and I said, as a doctor of divinity dragged me through the hall, "My dear doctor, what can I say about the Salvation Army that you have not heard already?"

"Well," he said, "come and tell us what we have heard. It will be interesting, more interesting than ever, to hear it from your lips."

That has been a great comfort to me since that day. It may be so here. (Applause.)

My time is limited, and I know it requires a man of more ability than I possess to make short speech that is of any service. An hour and a half or two hours is about my stent; and I have only got half an hour this morning. (Laughter.)

But the Salvation Army? How can I outline in a few words, so as to convey a succinct and distinct idea to your minds about it? And how can I say the things that you would like to know?

Well, it is 29 years of age. And yet I go further back and say sometimes it is 50 years old; that it was born with me; that it was inborn in my soul when God called me and changed me; when he showed me not only the evils of my own heart and the consequences of a life of transgression and the hollowness and emptiness of the world as an object of pursuit, but also showed me that I might be of some service to Him and some service to my generation. And those motives combined led me to His feet. I had nothing, you will perceive, to ask Him on behalf of myself, nothing from interested motives so far as my own experiences, my own individuality went, but I went with the offer of my poor services to Him in the great battle that I could see waging around me.

It was true that I was only a boy, only a lad of 15 years, and a lad who had then very little religious teaching or training. I knew next to nothing about my Bible, knew next to nothing about the mighty motives that urge men to lead a life of service and sacrifice; but I had come to see this, the hollowness of the world, so far as its satisfying capacity went; and I had come to see this, how much might be done through the power of God and through faithful service, to remove the sin and suffering that was round about me. Consequently, I gave myself right up and went to work right away on the lines on which the Salvation Army is traveling today.

As I say, I was then 15. God laid His afflicting hand upon me. I went down to the brink of the river and looked across to the eternities beyond. I rose from that bed, which appeared to me at the time to be the bed of death, and went forth, and without any instruction, without any hand or power behind me, sought out the lowest portion, the lowest parts of my native town; and there, standing on a chair, pleaded with the people on behalf of salvation, on behalf of lives of happiness and holiness. I pleaded with them for surrender of themselves to God.

It seemed to me that God wanted to impart Himself to the hearts of those who sought Him. It has always seemed to me, as it seemed then, that here is a man who has got away from God; in getting away from God, the moment he departs from God and God departs from him, he is driven out of paradise, away from the flowers, the music and joys and delights for which he was created, and driven out into the world of thistles and thorns and briers and sorrows and sicknesses and death and perdition; and that the only way he can possibly get back to paradise is by getting back to God.

And, therefore, I said, now, then, O ye poor people, O ye starving creatures, O ye poverty-stricken creatures, if you want to be relieved, if you want to be helped in your temporal affairs, and want to be helped altogether, come, ye prodigals, come home; in your Father's house there is enough and to spare. It always seemed to me, doctor, that if we could get the man inside put right, it would put the outside right, it would put his body right and put suitable clothes upon it, and put his habitation right, and put his circumstances right. (Applause) And, therefore, I said, let us put the man inside right, and invite these people to come to Jesus Christ.

And now, sir, I went forward on those lines for a considerable portion of time. Now, it seemed to me then, as it does now, a perfect marvel that those who have Christ within them, and what we might call the instincts and passions and purposes of Christ—that if Christ has been formed within a man, if there is Christ in the man, the man will love and hate and serve and suffer and sacrifice on the same lines that Christ suffered and sacrificed. That is, the Christ in him will manifest the Christ outside of him. Consequently, I started on those lines and went forward. You will mark that I was not in any shape or form encouraged particularly.

I was rather discouraged. The friends of decency and order inside the ecclesiastic institutions have never been very much my friends, have never been very friendly to my methods and my plans. They seem to be coming over now, but they have been a long while coming around. (Laughter and applause.) And at that very time I belonged to a very large and fashionable church, one with what you might call one of the most earnest and numerous memberships that I have ever come across. And yet, at that time, I was leading a procession of the ragtag and bobtail poor, wretched creatures up to this church. I received orders that they were all to be taken in at the back door, they could not be allowed to go in at the front door. But, sir, I persevered.

And then I became a preacher, that is, a lay preacher; and that had a very bad effect upon me. And then I became a minister, and that nearly finished me. (Laughter.) But, sir, I persevered, and then these old instincts were still in me. I was never satisfied with what I found inside the churches. I could not be satisfied with that spirit which it seemed to me existed. Perhaps it is not so in the United States, perhaps it is not so in Boston, perhaps it is not so in England at the present time. I do not think it is, to anything like the same extent. But there seemed to be an exclusiveness in the churches, there seemed to be a sort of two worlds, to me, a kind of church world and a kind of worldly world. And the worldly world got into the church very considerably in certain centers.

Then the church seemed to be in ignorance altogether of the ways and manners of the godless crowds who were outside. And the godless crowds outside were teetotally ignorant of the motives and methods and measures and purposes and loves and joys of the church world. Now, I wanted to go outside this church world, to go away from those walls, to go out among this devilish portion of the community, the reckless portion of the community. And, sir, after a long story, I went out.

And I went out with a wife, a delicate wife, who was one with me in the surrender, and one with me in the sacrifice, and stood up to me all the way from the first moment (applause)—from the first moment of our acquaintance; and if there was ever any feebleness manifested in my devotion, in my surrender, in my sacrifice, she strengthened me and pushed me forward. I went out with that precious companion and with four children, in order that I might get at this world in a better fashion. And I say this for the encouragement of any men or women here who are hesitating at any sacrifice that seems to lie in the way of their carrying out their vocation, the vocation of Christianity, which is to sacrifice yourselves for the salvation of your fellows—and you cannot get at the salvation of your fellows without sacrificing yourselves in some form or other.

And to any man or any woman who is hesitating here as to what is going to come to him or her, what is going to happen, I want to say, before I had gone outside three weeks, when I left those doors, and left behind me, as a Methodist preacher, as I had to leave behind me everything I had, and go almost naked out into the world, not knowing who would be my friends—for the friends I had looked upon me as a fanatic, if not as a fool—before I had been working three weeks, we were on the crest of one of the mightiest waves of salvation that had ever reached that part of the country, the products of which have been putting out their hands to bless me and welcome me to every part of the world to which I am going at the present time. (Applause.)

I went out in this fashion. And then I came and found there was a lower depth still, when I came to that grand city, that great metropolitan center of London, and came to the eastern portion of it, where they told me that within a mile's circumference of the spot on which I stood, within a mile's circumference in that city, there was something like a million of people, 90 percent of whom had never crossed the threshold of any church or of any mission, and who were as ignorant of the gospel plan as the inhabitants of Africa or the cannibals of the far-away seas. I looked at these people on Saturday afternoon.

Misery and Satan always had a fascination, misery and sin in their extreme have a fascination for all good men. Misery and sin in their extreme have a fascination for the angels of heaven; misery and sin in their extreme had a fascination for the Son of God and brought him down from heaven in order that he might seek to recover that which was lost. (Applause.) It attracted me. But this was only the working out of Christian instincts. I lay claim to nothing peculiar, sir. Was I not a friend of God? Was I not a son of God? Do I not know the Spirit of God is witnessing within me? The witness of the Spirit is God's Spirit witnessing to my spirit that I am a child of God, and making me know it.

Now, sir, just in passing, let me touch on this tempting theme. If you ask me how I know I am alive this morning, how I know that I am in possession of animal life, of the life that is in my frame, well, I might say, how could I have talked to 20,000 people yesterday in that Mechanics Hall, except I had been alive; how can I come here this morning and talk to you, except I was alive? I know I am alive because I do the work of a living man. But then, if I wanted to satisfy myself I am alive, I have a much shorter cut than that. I know I am. Nobody can persuade me out of it. I know I am alive. And just so in my spiritual relationships.

Everyone who has been born of God, and has that life within his soul, says, "I am alive, because I can do the works which only a man born of God could do." And more than that, he says, "I know I am. I feel it. It is with me every hour and every day, the consciousness of my divine relationship, of my possession of this spirit, of my hopes, my assurance in regard to the eternal world, and this is wrought in me by the possession of the Spirit."

"He that is born of the flesh is flesh, and he that is born of the Spirit is spirit." He has the spiritual life. Sir, that is a mighty theme that needs pushing upon the attention of the churches today. I have been musing, musing, musing this very morning on the great want of certainty, the indefinite way in which multitudes of people live in regard to their spiritual relationship. How few there are who stand up and say, "Yes, glory be to God." They like to leave that out, because it is "Salvation Army." How few there are that can say, "Yes, I know, I can feel that I am; it is not merely I hope so. I have it, and I know this is the case."

But to go back again. I came to London, and there, when I looked at these people, I said, "These people are sheep without a shepherd. Can something be done for them?" And I gave myself up to them. I separated myself, cut myself off, as I thought, forever from any church, from any church organization, and, as I supposed, from any work along other lines. When men go out for God, they never know where God is going to lead them. They never know what sort of Canaan He is going to bring them to die in, even if they have to go into the wilderness to get there. I went into the wilderness. And so far as the friendship of good and great and blessed men is concerned, I went out and traveled many a year, many a weary, weary, weary year, in the face of persecution and slanders and ridicule and hatred.

But now, sir, I feel, when I get to Boston, as if I was going to end my days in Canaan, after all. (Laughter and applause.)

So I went to work. I gave myself to those people, and began to talk to them. Now the difficulty came. How was I going to reach them? There I stood in the face of this crowd. I had no one to help me. I had no powerful corporation, no rich corporation behind me to furnish me with funds, no powerful religious corporation to furnish me with agencies. It is true a handful of people gathered around me at the outset, for my reputation had preceded me, and a few of the saints who lived around about walked a long distance and came down to help me for the first few days; but they soon grew weary when they had been marching in the streets and traveling through the mud, to be cursed and persecuted and to meet that which is the most difficult thing in the world for a man to endure, ridicule and laughter and sneers, and they forsook me and fled.

But, after all that time, I had got a couple of fellows with me, one to keep the door, and the other to make the collection. And I had the platform. (Laugher and applause.)

Then difficulties began to multiply. They asked me where I was going to get my leaders. I said, "Out of the saloons." And I have got some wonderfully clever fellows out of saloons. (Applause.) I have got some there, sir, that I would not change for any doctors of divinity you could find me. (Laughter and applause.) And then they asked me what I was going to do with my converts. And I said I would send them to the churches. But then, sir, three difficulties appeared in the way: First, they wouldn't go when I sent them. Secondly, they were not wanted when they went. And thirdly, I wanted them myself. (Loud laughter and applause.)

Then they increased and increased and increased, as all real life does increase. When it does not increase, it is not life at all. It must spread itself out. There may be great feebleness in service, there may be a Laodicean condition of things in the churches, so that you cannot say that the condition is that of absolute death, and yet they do not increase. At any rate, we increased; we were alive.

Then I was faced with the question, Are you going to make another religious denomination? Now, this was directly opposed, diametrically opposed, to all my notions. I had been opposed to the idea from the very beginning. I always thought there were sadly too many. (Applause.) My time is nearly gone, leave the clapping to the last. I thank you very much, though. It cheers a fellow on, especially in this country (laughter), where you don't get too much, for it is often like talking in a museum to a lot of petrified people. But to go on, I said to myself that if I had had the ability and had not had another calling, I would have offered myself as an apostle of union and gone through the world trying to persuade the organizations to come together, for whom no reason could have been given in heaven or on earth for their remaining apart.

Now, here I was on the eve of forming another religious organization. I struggled against it. I made desperate efforts for a union with all the existing organizations. They received me at the onset with very great favor, with very great favor indeed, and I thought we were going to have great success. But then, afterward, we met with some of the dried-up old fogies who would rather reign in a certain place than serve another (laughter), and they saw there were great difficulties, and perhaps the greatest difficulty they foresaw was the difficulty of managing General Booth. (Renewed laughter.) But anyway, sir, the thing fell through.

And even in after days, sir, when churches, when organizations, when the most powerful organizations now, perhaps, in the world, anyway in the Old World, although they have their representatives here, sought me out and said, "Can't we comprehend you" when bishops and archbishops and presidents and leaders of those organizations wished to put their sheltering arms around about us and unite us with them, it was too late then for such a union. I was afraid it would not be possible. I do not know what it will be in the future.

I said to the present archbishop of Canterbury, who was then bishop of Truro, and to the present bishop of Durham, who was then dean of something, I forget what for the moment, these gentlemen waited upon me, and when they invited me to join them I said, "No, I do not think we can run on the same road and in the same community, but we can be like two streams running side by side, with plenty of bridges—I got rather mixed up, you see—with plenty of bridges, so we can cross over. You can come over to us, and we will help you with our freedom from conventionalities and with our enthusiasm, and we can come over to you and get some instruction from you and a good collection." (Laughter) I said, "I think we shall be the most likely to help each other in that fashion." It is going to be so, I think, and it is to be so with the churches.

But, sir, it is passed along until we have come to what we are today, a mighty, powerful force, created by the Spirit of God through and for the Glory of God, a body of people combined after the fashion—not in imitation, but after the fashion of a military force. I say not by imitation, but God brought us to that; and when we found we had got an army, that he had used us to make an army, we called it an army. And as it was an army for the deliverance of men from the domination of evil, the mastership of the devil, we called it the army of deliverance, the Army of Salvation; and it is today, "the Salvation Army."

Well, sir, I say, as I said Saturday afternoon, we have pushed our way and are pushing our way into the uttermost corners of the earth. God has been very good to me. He has given me great helpers. He gave me a helper whose value is beyond human enumeration, is beyond, I was almost going to say, conception, in my precious wife; and He has raised up around me children who are one in heart and one in soul with me, with no other ambition, no other aim, but to build up, to make this force what it seems to them God wants it to be. And he has raised around me a body of men, also, and of women, of equal ability and equal devotion, ever increasing.

There are thousands and thousands of mothers and fathers who are training their children and nursing them in that idea, go forth and fight for the King of Kings and fight for the bodies and souls of men, a fight which will involve them in poverty and sorrow and trouble and difficulty; and, as far as that goes, involve them, as may be, in death. And while God has kept us up to the present hour, my encouragement for the future is the growing spirit of self-sacrifice, the growing desire to follow men and women in their sorrows to the still lower depths. And I believe this is not only going to be continued, but to grow still further.

And now, sir, I have been asked to answer two or three questions, and my time is up. Will you read them out, doctor, although I am afraid I shall not be able to answer them.

Dr. Cook: What proportion of the population that you reach is lifted into a favorable position of life under the action of the Salvation Army? What proportion of the submerged tenth emerges?

General Booth: A very large proportion. I shall deal with some statistics with respect to this matter, statistics carefully compiled, in regard to those who come under the operations of our social scheme, tomorrow night. But I have no doubt and think I can say in passing, with regard to the results of all the operations of our army in the poorer neighborhoods where they work, not only are remarkable results obtained in the case of those who become soldiers, but in the general influence in the community, for men and women saved from the lower depths of sin have a mighty effect upon the whole mass of people who live around them.

Dr. Cook: You will excuse our asking this question in Boston: What would be the practical effect on the work of the Salvation Army of preaching the doctrine or hypothesis of probation after death, or annihilation of the wicked?

General Booth: If you were to take hell out of our doctrine, the Salvation Army would soon disappear. (Laughter and applause)

Dr. Cook: The last question is: What religious truths and doctrines have been most blessed in the work of the Salvation Army?

General Booth: Making men feel the evil of sin. Perhaps there are no people under heaven who work more upon that one idea that sin is an evil, a devilish thing, that is destroying the happiness, present and prospective, of those with whom we talk; that with sin they have got hell with them, and if they do not get saved from their sins, they will go to hell forever. And that makes an impression upon the poor, and upon the rich, also, when people say it who believe it.

Appendix B

William Booth's Prayer in the United States Senate, February 12, 1903.

O Lord God, our Heavenly Father, maker, sustainer and governor of all things, we, Thy servants, the work of Thy hands, come into Thy presence this morning to supplicate Thy blessing upon ourselves, upon those dependent upon us, and the world round about us.

We acknowledge before Thee our obligations for all the good things that we enjoy. Thy goodness and Thy mercy have followed each one of us all the days of our lives, and are flowing around us at the present moment. Thou hast not only made us, and clothed us, and housed us, and befriended us, and provided ways and means by which, though we may have fallen from Thy sight, and given ourselves up to doing things that have brought down upon ourselves the exposure to Thy just displeasure, yet Thou hast made a wonderful way and a wonderful contrivance by which we can be regulated, can be saved, and can be rescued from the circumstances in which we find ourselves. Thou hast made salvation and happiness, goodness and truth and love possible to us here and possible to us in the world to come.

We thank Thee, we adore Thee, we worship Thee. We not only acknowledge our obligation, but we desire to make some suitable response to it. In what we feel in our innermost hearts, in what we think about these matters, no response can be accepted by Thee but what is to be satisfactory to our own conscience and our own judgment here and hereafter, by the rendering of ourselves up as willing sacrifices, and the carrying out of Thy wishes, and the doing of Thy blessed will.

We thank Thee that Thou hast made it possible for each one of us, when we pray as individuals, to feel the light and truth and power of Thy Holy Spirit, and that through the sacrifices of our Lord we may not only see what we ought to do, but be directed through it not only to begin but to finish, that we may have satisfaction in the last moments of earth and not be discouraged.

And now, Lord, we pray for this great nation, for this great heart of hearts of this mighty country—the very center of its activities, the place where it exercises its power and its strength. We pray for Thy blessing on this great nation. We thank Thee for all Thy goodness to it, and that through Thy loving-kindness it may be not only great and capable of promoting the highest degree of happiness and well-being of its own people, but that it may by Thy great grace be made a great power in the world, and make a glorious stand for righteousness and truth and peace and happiness among the nations.

To this end we pray for Thy servant who at the present time is placed at its head; for him and for his family, and for all associated with him; that he may have wisdom and benevolence and courage to enable him to discharge the great and solemn duties that have devolved upon him.

We pray Thy blessing for the men who sit in this and the adjacent chambers, that the men here will reason, that the men here will think, that the men here will plan, that the men here will seek only compliance on those measures and opinions which are wisest and best. Oh, may they seek Thy wisdom and may they rely on Thy great arm, and may the results of their deliberations end in the direction of Thy glory and the good of mankind. Remember the people that are more or less influenced by them; and while they are considering matters that are for the welfare of this great people, may they not only consider those who are so circumstanced and environed as to be able to secure those conditions of life that are essential to health and morality and religion, but may they remember those who have perhaps, properly speaking, no representative to voice their sorrows and their toils and their cares. Remember, in Thy infinite mercy, these poor and lost members of the community, and may Thy blessing be upon us all.

May we do our work, may we do it well, may we do it with satisfaction to our own consciences and satisfaction to our laws, so that when we meet again we shall meet in the center of the government of the universe before the Great Throne, and we may have the satisfaction of hearing Thee say to us individually and to those we love, our families, our wives and children: "Well done, thou good and faithful servant . . . enter thou into the joy of the Lord." For Jesus Christ's sake, our Savior, who saves us now and all the time, and evermore.